MW00769145

Broken and Beautiful
From Ashes to Beauty Rising

Liz Liles

FIRE TOWER
MEDIA

Broken and Beautiful: From Ashes to Beauty Rising
Copyright © 2018 by Liz Liles. All rights reserved.

Cover photograph copyright © Fire Tower Media. All rights reserved.
Cover background image copyright © Fire Tower Media. All rights reserved.
Book design by Michael Sharpe

Scripture quotations are from the Holy Bible, English Standard Version,
copyright © 2001 by Crossway Bibles, a publishing ministry of good News
Publishers. Used by permission. All rights reserved.

ISBN 978-1-7323193-0-1

Published by Fire Tower Media, Inc.
www.firetowermedia.com

This book is dedicated to every girl who has every silently wished that she could simply be more....
Beautiful girl,
You Already Are.

ACKNOWLEDGMENTS

To my Grace-Giver, Hope Whisperer, Lover of my Soul, I am so thankful for your relentless love and authentic grace. Without you, I am nothing.

For the family who gave me the sweet gift of breath and life and for the family who gave me a home – a place to belong … thank you for your love that sustains.

To the boys who made me a mom – who have taught me how to love beyond reason and who are the very reason my heart beats, you will always and forever be my babies.

To the precious kiddos who have taught me what adoption truly is – to love another in such a way, even though they do not physically belong to you – you teach me every day to love more and to laugh and live fully! Thank you!

To my soul mate and best friend, my warrior and advocate… I am eternally grateful for you. Thank you for your love – for believing in me – even and especially when I doubt myself.

To my tribe… You are the ones. You are truly my people. The ones who hold me tight in heart and prayer – who strengthen and encourage me each day. We share deep laughter over coffee and spill tears over wine. You are the strong – fierce – warrior – army tribe that I have waited my entire life for – and I am so incredibly thankful for each and every one of you! You know who you are… and you know that Daughters of Worth would simply not even exist without you! Thank you for joining me as we fight for the girls of our communities together!

To my girls… GLAM girls of Daughters of Worth, you are sunshine in my days and the fire of my soul! You are the ones that I dream of meeting years from now to discover that you are truly our beautiful, strong, smart, classy, compassionate, generous, faithful community and government leaders who are simply transforming lives with your every step, action, and word! Beautiful girls, I believe in You! And you are so very loved, treasured and adored more than you will ever even know!

To my readers, the broken and the beautiful, may you find healing for your heart and redemption for your souls and beauty for all of the ashes from the One who gives grace to all and who simply delights in You! Beautiful one, You are So Very Loved!

INTRODUCTION

For years, she had listened to the voice. To the voices that others had whispered to her throughout the years.

Not pretty enough.
Not smart enough.
Not talented enough.
Not popular enough.
Not thin enough.
Not athletic enough.
Not wealthy enough.
Just. Not. Enough.

These voices – these murmurings seemed to be locked in her heart and etched in her mind. They didn't play each and every day, but when they did – they chose her most vulnerable moments. They chose the days that she struggled the most. The days where she just could not find the strength to fight. And in these moments, they would whisper into the quiet places of her soul…That she didn't have what it takes, that she wouldn't be able to succeed, that she wasn't capable or worthy of being fully loved – without measure or condition, that she would always have to settle with simply not being enough. And she listened so intently – for so very long – that soon, she began to believe them.

Yet, there comes this Day.

There comes this day where is a beautiful Hope Arising, an Awakening of the Soul, and the Ashes of our Lives – the broken dreams, the failed promises, the painful memories suddenly begin to vanish. They are blown away by the Great Spirit, the Giver of Life and Love. And in this very moment…
Beauty is found.
Redemption draws near.
Hope springs forth!

The Love-Giver redeems the broken pieces of our lives, gathering them into His Nail-Scarred Hands and Breathes His Breath of Grace and Redemption upon it all. In a place where only rubble had remained, there is now a new creation!

And it is absolutely Beautiful!

The story-line that others had determined was insufficient, ineligible, and unworthy has now been repurposed for a magnificent calling in only the way that Grace can offer. A place where Grace breaks in and releases you from captivity. And for most of us, we never even realized that we were in bondage.

Until that Day comes.

For those of you who are like me, and have found yourselves lost in the rubble…You look around and all you can see is the devastating aftermath of a life that somehow went terribly wrong. The life that you had imagined would be yours is nowhere in sight, and restoration appears impossible.

For those of you who are in the broken place of failed dreams, shattered hopes, raging waters that you cannot seem to calm and voices that you cannot silence, this book is written for you.

It is a story of Love and Grace. It is where Beauty and Brokenness collide. It is where story lines are redeemed before our first breath and where Hope breaks every boundary to come and make Love Known! It is where the Creator of Life and Love comes to dwell with us, so that we can be healed… restored…. And deliver others.

There is truly something beautifully raw when we choose to be broken, for the sake of being restored. And this is the journey that we must be willing to pursue – if we truly want to be healed from the remnants of failed dreams and enter into the Life that was designed specifically for us by the Giver of Grace.

If you are ready to exchange your perception for His reality, your wishes for His dreams, your brokenness for His wholeness, your weaknesses for His strength, your ashes for His beauty... then I welcome you with open arms and a full heart to the beginning of our journey together.

"The Spirit of the Sovereign Lord is on me, because the Lord has anointed me to proclaim the good news to the poor. He has sent me to bind up the brokenhearted, to proclaim freedom for the captives and release from darkness for the prisoners, to proclaim the year of the Lord's favor and the day of vengeance of our God, to comfort all who mourn, and provide for those who grieve in Zion – to bestow on them a crown of beauty instead of ashes, the oil of joy instead of mourning, and a garment of praise instead of a spirit of despair. They will be called oaks of righteousness, a planting of the Lord for the display of His splendor." Isaiah 61:1

"For my frame was not hidden from you when I was being made in secret." Psalm 139:15

1:FAMILY SECRETS

He was twenty-six years old. She was sixteen. They had been together for nearly a year and a half, and she just knew that their story was going to offer the magical happily ever after that she had longed for and dreamed of sharing with him. She truly thought that he was her Knight in shining armor, her Prince Charming, her love for life.

The only problem was (and it was a fairly significant one) that he was already committed to another woman as her Happily Ever After. He was a married man with four beautiful daughters of his own, and she was a 16 year old preacher's daughter who had just learned that all of her hopes had failed.

There I was growing in the secret place of her womb while she watched her entire life begin to crumble away. This was certainly not the end that she had envisioned for her life. This was not the way this whole love and baby thing was supposed to go down.

How had she missed all of this.

With her every breath, she had honestly believed that he was "the one." Never in a million years would she have expected to learn that this entire time – this entire relationship – had been founded and fueled on lies. Deceit. Mistrust. Deception. Rejection. She was a girl scorned by the love of her life, and I was the product of an affair. I was the product of shame. I was the end result of infidelity.

This was the place that I was created from, or so I believed for many years. And these lies of the enemy that would whisper ever so gently into my soul in my weakest places had the power to bring me down to my lowest – to a place that I believed I couldn't escape.

With my every breath, I fully believe that there are hundreds of thousands of women who are just like me. They have been chained to the voice and lies of the enemy, locked in a mental and emotional prison. They are continuing to partake of the toxin directly from the hand of the enemy. And all because we have believed the lie.

We have believed the lie that because we were not conceived in wedlock, or we were not loved from our families, or we were somehow rejected and abandoned… that we are a mistake.

We actually never speak these words out loud, but we tuck this mindset, this soul belief directly down into the core of our very being and in our lives that we live out each day, we hear this echo:

"You are not good enough."

"You are not loved."

"No one wants you."

It is this very lie that plunges us to do everything in our will-house to somehow make ourselves more loveable – more beautiful – more creative – more intelligent – more successful – more desirable – more…. More… MORE.

And in this place of "more-ness," the second lie that we lock and latch on to is that no matter how much we do or serve or give or buy or sacrifice or try – that it's never enough. That We are Never Enough.

For those of you who are like me and are completely drained and exhausted with this weary life of placating, nursing, and carrying around this self-sabotaging belief, this lie from the pit of Hell… that you are not loved or wanted or valuable or enough… this book is for you.

Because here is the thing…. After 37 years of allowing this joy-sucking lie to pry itself into literally every single corner of my life, I have finally chosen to allow the truth and the power of the One who created me – who created you – who formed us and planned us and loves us and delivers us – to come into the dark shadows of this lie-infested heart and soul arena and to clean house with the power and authority of His Word!

Beautiful one, we are no longer slaves to sin. We are no longer captives of the originator of lies. We are the beloved of the Great I AM.

And these are His words to us...

"For you formed my inward parts. You knitted me together in my mother's womb. I praise you for I am fearfully and wonderfully made. Wonderful are your works; my soul knows it very well." Psalm 139:14

Precious girl, do not miss this! Rejoice in these truths with me!

1. God formed us. He knit us together in our mother's womb! The world may say that we are a mistake because of affairs or unexpected pregnancies or rape or unforeseen circumstances, but it is truly the One who created the entire Universe – all things – who knit us together Himself! This is just the most precious gift ever!

2. We praise Him because we are fearfully and wonderfully made. You are a wonderful and beautiful creation of the King, Our Lord! He has poured talents, skills, abilities, gift and beauty into your very soul to be used for an extraordinary purpose! In fact, He even declares in Ephesians 2:10 that we are His workmanship, created in Christ Jesus and that we have been created for good works! Precious girl, you are Not a mistake!

3. His works are wonderful, and we are a product of His creation, His plan, and His design. There is absolutely nothing about you, your beginning or your life story that is a mistake. He is working it all to the good of those who love Him, who are called according to His purpose! (Romans 8:28)

For so many years, I cuddled with the lies of the enemy – and didn't even realize what I was doing. I embedded them into my heart and etched them into my mind. I recited the words that he fed me, and I believed them. Every relationship, goal, and dream was met with the resistance and the lie of "Not being good enough." For 37 years, I have allowed this lie – the enemy – to deflate my confidence, disable my dreams, to sabotage relationships, and to rob me of joy because I chose to digest the voice the enemy rather than to taste of the goodness of the voice of my God, my Creator.

Beautiful one, it's time for us to step up and to take back our lives – to dispose of the toxin from our hearts and souls – and to become restored by the Giver, the Creator of our lives.

Pause and meditate on the truths of His heart, the love that He so desires to lavish upon you today. For He rejoices in you! He delights in you with singing! (Zephaniah 3:17) He wants you to hear these words and to imprint this love-letter in your heart:

"Beloved one, you are loved. You are wanted. You are treasured. You are enough. You are truly Worth More. Exactly as you are. You don't have to pretend or work harder or try to be anyone any different. You are exactly enough. Exactly as you are. Just come to Me and know that you are loved."

Love, the Creator of Your Soul –

"Your eyes saw my unformed substance; in your book were written, every one of them, the days that were formed for me, when as yet there was none of them." Psalm 139:16

2:UNWANTED

When you are a 16-year-old girl with a family knee-deep in the Bible belt and your daddy is a Pentecostal Holiness Evangelist, coming home to share that you are now expecting a baby and there is no hope for a future with the baby-daddy is quite terrifying! Generally, babies out of wedlock, laced with adultery are not too highly favored in the religious community and can quickly result in the catastrophic demise of a once hopeful ministry.

In an urgent resolve to protect the family name and even more, to safe guard the hope of a successful and prosperous ministry, the decision was made to give me away. No one would ever even breathe mention of this "incident." In fact, it would be even better if no one outside of the family even knew anything about what had taken place.

The plans had been set. They would take their daughter to Florence Crittenton, a maternity home in Charlotte, NC, and she would reside there until the baby was born.

Immediately upon birth, this 16 year old would sign the formal papers to end it all. Her rights would be relinquished. The baby would become an orphan. The family would reclaim its status. No one would ever even have to know that this "incident" had occurred. No harm, no foul.

Of all of the lies that have tormented me throughout the years, this is The One that has caused my soul to grieve and my heart to bleed fear more times than I can even count.

The words.... "If your own mother didn't love you enough to keep you, how do you expect anyone else to?"

"You weren't even good enough at birth to be kept. What makes you think you are good enough now?"

"If your own family – Your own blood line – can look at you, keep you a secret, deny you ever even existed and give you away to strangers – then how do you actually expect anyone else to stay?"

No matter how hard I tried to counteract these thoughts, to bury them or to at least shut them up when none of the above worked, these thoughts just never seemed to disappear. They were like the puppy who follows you from room to room, always wanting to sit with you when you stop for a moment and making certain that you are always aware of its presence. Only these thoughts were not anywhere as loving, joyful and desirable as a puppy!

It has taken me a long time to get to this point, and please let me assure you that I am definitely still a work in progress! This voice, these thoughts of being a secret, of not being wanted are still there. They haven't magically disappeared, although I wish that they would.

But what I am learning is that I have the power and the ability to silence the thoughts.

And it has Nothing to do with me – and Everything to do with the One who not only formed me and created me, but who knows me and who loves me. Even when it's difficult for me to love myself.

Listen to these precious words:

"Your eyes saw my unformed substance; in your book were written, every one of them, the days that were formed for me, when as yet there was none of them." Psalm 139:16

Beautiful girl, I don't know your story. I don't know the places in your life that bring you to tears, and I don't know the voices that you want to bury or at least silence. But what I do know is this... the Giver of Love and Life has a Master vision and plan for you and for me since before the creation of the world, and we are a part of it! In His eyes, we have Never been a mistake. We have Always been wanted. And not only are we part of the plan, He created us with the plan in mind!

Before we ever even took our first breath, in His Book were written – every one of them – the days written for me and for you. And this is the very place where my soul finds peace. Joy. Redemption.

He didn't just buy me back from sin through the Cross! He redeemed my birth story before I had ever even taken my first breath! He gave me hope – life – a name – and a story before I ever even realized that it was missing!

Regardless of the fact that my blood line felt that they had to protect the name and ministry by keeping me a secret and placing me for adoption, my frame was truly Never hidden! His eyes saw me and knew me. He was devising a Master plan that would involve many more people, and this was all a part of His plan to fulfill His mission for the calling and purpose that He had poured into me. Even before the creation of the world!

The story line was not by accident.

The family that He needed to give me life and the family that He needed to give me a home could not be the same.

Every piece of this puzzle was orchestrated by Love and for the purpose of Love so that others could find Hope!

Sometimes it is easy for us to tangle ourselves in the perceptions, belief, emotions that we have about a situation or circumstance – especially when it directly involves our lives.

Yet, as we begin to step back from our personal bias and look deep into the heart of our God through His life changing Word, we find that we are simply an expression of His Love, and every single part of our story (the beautiful and the broken) are all to be offered for His glory and can all be redeemed through His grace.

We simply must allow His love to come and heal our deepest wounds and to silence the voice of the enemy through the power and authority of His Truth.

"How precious to me are your thoughts, O God! How vast is the sum of them!" Psalm 17

3: THE MASTER DESIGNER OF LIVES

For 4 years, they had diligently tried to expand their family – and failed. While others around them were celebrating their successful two line test and planning baby showers, decorating nurseries, and shopping for pink or blue, this couple grieved. It was in the quiet nights of their home that they questioned why God had not chosen them to be parents. They were good people, and they were well respected in the community. They strived daily to live with integrity, to love God, to love others. They were not wealthy, but hard work and discipline had taught them how to manage their finances well and how to live comfortably, but within their means.

Yet, for whatever reason, none of this seemed to be enough to qualify them for "mom and dad" in the realm of the Universe giving of parenthood.

Doctor appointments were made. Tests were taken. Examinations were experienced. All of this in a desperate attempt to earn the gift of the pitter-patter of little feet, sleepless nights, late nights and early mornings, school projects and ear infections. Yet, more than anything, they wanted to have a baby. To be a family. To experience the gift of children at home.

Finally, the news came. The news that they had feared and dreaded all within the same breath. The news that they were deemed ineligible. The world of science and biology had no grace. The answer was simply "No." No apology. No insight. No justification. Just "No."

In that moment, every hope of a woman who longs to carry her own child – to experience midnight cravings and the growing of the enormous belly, to decorate the nursery and to give birth –

was snatched from her hands with no mercy attached. Science could not change it. Life could not change it.

But God could. And He would. And He did.

It would just take place in a different way than they had originally planned or expected.

Yet, He was not surprised at all.

It was all a part of the story – the Master Plan – that He was orchestrating beautifully. In a way that only He could do. Where lives remain intact, hearts are restored, and dreams are redeemed.

It was the story of Love being played out. His most favorite theme of all!

And the story was being written by the Creator of Love Himself!

In Romans 8:28, the Love-Giver shares these words with us: "And we know that all things work together for the good of those who love Him, and those who are called according to His purpose."

In the gut-wrenching crisis of failed dreams, robbed hopes, unplanned events, family secrets, shameful mistakes and detoured lives, it's incredibly easy for us to come to the conclusion that we must have really screwed up something significant to now be here – in this place.

Yet, what is truly happening… is we are being prepared for a greater work. Our story has a much larger impact – a more powerful significance than we can even begin to imagine! We are created to love God, to love others, and to share this Love with the world!

Yet, if we don't believe that our lives have been created with passion and purpose… if we don't believe that we have been stitched together with Love… if we don't believe that we have a purpose, a plan, and a vision, it's certainly difficult to inspire and encourage others in their journey. And it's nearly impossible to declare the goodness of the Lord if we are silently questioning His motives for our own lives.

Our Creator is a God of love, peace, joy, and order. Everything that He does exemplifies these qualities to the fullest extent possible! He already knows the course that we are going to take, and He graciously allows us to choose our own path. However, He also loves us enough to redirect our paths, to restore our souls, and to create good out of the situations that we have no idea how to correct on our own.

The Love-Giver knew that on June 23, 1980, I would enter this world at Charlotte Memorial Hospital and would essentially become an orphan within hours. He knew that I would need a home with a family who would embrace me with unconditional love, grace, acceptance, and who would offer bountiful patience (especially during my teen years!)

He also knew that in Elizabeth City, NC, there was a young couple who desperately wanted to be parents. This young Coach and Athletic Director was unable to provide the love of his life, his soul mate, his best friend , his beautiful wife with the one treasure that she wanted more than anything in this world – a baby.

Only the God of Love – the Creator of the Universe – could take these two families who had never met and intertwine their stories in such a beautiful way that all of the broken would be restored. Only the God of Love could write a story where each family was able to find healing, grace, and redemption – where dreams that had been severely damaged and utterly destroyed were able to be resurrected and given the Breath of Life through His Hope. Through His power alone.

And here is the beautiful thing about our God… He isn't a God who chooses favorites or discriminates – only allowing specific people to receive His favor and mercy. He offers the invitation to each and every one of us. We simply must choose to come to the party of Love! He is already working on your behalf and writing your story! He is simply waiting for you to receive the invitation that He has left for you at the door of your life and to come receive the gift of Love and Hope that is anxiously awaiting your arrival!

What are the places in your life that seem to be broken beyond repair?

What are the dreams and hopes that you have embedded in your heart for years and now seems to be ripped apart – and you have absolutely no control?

Maybe it's the marriage that you tried diligently to save, but you couldn't make it work, and shame lingers every corner you turn.

Maybe it's the child who has chosen his or her own path. Regardless of how much you try to love them, nurture them, and guide them in the right direction – they refuse your efforts, they reject you.

Maybe you are expecting a baby and you didn't anticipate this ending for your life… or you are like my mom, you have been wanting a baby – a family for so long – and your prayers haven't been answered.

I don't know what crushed dreams that you are staring at this very moment or what prayer that you are so patiently/anxiously awaiting for the Lord to hear and redeem, but what I do know is this:

You are Loved, and you have not been forgotten. Jeremiah 29:11-13 is one of my cherished scriptures. For it declares, "For I know the plans that I have for you, declares the Lord, plans for welfare and not for evil, to give you a future and a hope. Then you will call upon me and come and pray to me, and I will hear you. You will seek me and find me, when you seek me with all your heart."

Precious one, hear and receive the beauty and power and delightfully glorious grace-full promises of the Creator of our Lives!

The plans for you and for your life are KNOWN by the creator of the world! Not only are you a part of the plan – His plan – which again, emphasizes that we are Not mistakes (Praise!)…. But he also has a Plan for us and for our lives individually.

This plan is for welfare and Not for evil. This plan is Intended to give us a Hope and a Future! What a precious gift! His whole heart just oozes love, hope, grace, and mercy in all things that He creates, designs, orchestrates and implements! We are created with the intent and purpose of having a life filled with joy, purpose, power, hope and a future! I just love this!

He hears us. He listens to us. And we can find Him. I think that sometimes when we are in the middle of the chaotic trenches of unanswered prayers and failed dreams, we somehow think that our prayers just didn't make it. He didn't actually hear us. Maybe too many mistakes were in the way. Our voices were drowned out by our bad decisions. Yet, once again, these are all tactics of the evil one to lead us astray and to force us to resign our hope and trust in Him.

Precious one, our heart whispers are not lost in the wind. He hears our soul prayers, our heart-wrenching pleas for help. Even before we speak them. "Even before a word is on my tongue, behold, O Lord, you know it altogether." (Psalm 139:4)

And as we chase after the Lover of our souls, the Master Designer of our lives, the Redeemer of our eternity, we find Him. Him. Jesus. Not a counterfeit or a "stand in." We find Jesus. And He makes Himself Known. It is here, in this very place that the Creator of Love does the very thing that He does best... He restores.

He restores our soul, bringing our burdened hearts under His care and exchanging our grief for His rest... our sorrow for His joy. (Matthew 11:28-30)

In Him, we find peace.
In Him, we find rest.
In Him, we find love.
In Him, we find our hope and our future.
In Him, we find our true worth.

"I give them eternal life, and they will never perish, and no one will snatch them out of My hand. My Father, who has given them to me is greater than all, and no one is able to snatch them out of the Father's hand. I and the Father are one."

John 10:28-30

4: THE HEART OF THE LOVE-GIVER

At 3:22pm on June 23, 1980, I gasped my first breath of air of life and cried my very first tears. My birth mother held me in her arms, meeting her baby daughter for the very first time.

She would have never expected that she would have a baby at this age – in this way – in this place. Soon, they would come to take me away – and she would be left with empty arms and a devastated heart.

In all honesty, she had not wanted to place me for adoption. But there was no choice allowed. It would ruin the ministry. It would pollute the family name. There was too much at stake, and with five children already in the home, there wasn't room for another. She knew this. She knew that they were not ready for a baby granddaughter no more than she was actually ready to be a mother. Nevertheless, the facts didn't lessen the pain.

The decision had been made.

The papers were signed.

It was only a matter of time before the agency would arrive to pick up the orphan child and deliver her to her new temporary home.

For nine months, we had shared the same body. We had connected and bonded from mother to baby in womb in the way that only maternal mothers can understand. She had loved, cared for, and protected me against the world for as long as she was allowed. And I had entrusted her to bring me into this world safely, which she did.

15

But within a matter of moments, everything changed forever as the worker reached into her nurturing arms to remove me from her lap and from her life.

In this simple gesture, we had transitioned from mother and daughter to biological mother and orphan.

We came to this place together, but we would leave as strangers.

In the very same place where we connected and looked into each other's eyes for the very first time, we would also say goodbye and depart to separate lives. The place where birth certificates are amended, names are changed, and all identifying information is erased as if it never even existed in the first place.

I would be transported to a foster home in Greensboro, NC and wait for the adoption to be finalized before meeting my permanent new family. She would leave for her new home in Sanford, NC with all of the outward appearance of a brand new mom, but with no baby to love and nurture.

It was a life that neither of us had chosen to make our own. Yet, it was all a part of the beautiful plan. One that neither of us would come to understand until many years later.

And this is exactly how the beautiful and broken often displays itself. At the time, we cannot even possibly begin to understand how anything good and glorious can come out of a complete hot mess! Yet, the Creator of all good things has a specialty - and this is it! Restoration.

So many times, people, possessions, opportunities, and careers are snatched out of our hands. And for many of us — it wasn't anything that we wanted or agreed to. It just happened. Maybe it was a decision that someone else made for us, and we had no choice in the matter. Maybe it was a tragedy in life that no explanation that can even be offered. Maybe it was a dream that was so close to being tangible that you can taste it, and suddenly, without warning, it all crumbled away.

If this is you, please know that you are not alone.

Because I had "learned" at a very young age that I was disposable, a secret, abandoned, not wanted, and could be taken away at any moment from people who were supposed to love and protect me, I created an incredibly strong "safe wall" within my heart.

Though I loved people, I would only allow certain ones to be close – and even then, I would proceed with intense caution. I entered every friendship and relationship with the preconceived notion that soon, they would also leave.

Creating self –fulfilling prophecies such as these for yourself is never a good idea! We think that we are protecting our hearts, but we are actually damaging our lives and hindering our future. We aren't enjoying the beauty and fullness of joy that loving others and embracing friendships can provide for our parched souls!

I missed so many years of truly developing meaningful and sustainable relationships because I was anxiously anticipating the exodus. It was easier to believe that if I chose to safeguard against love and friendship and not allow others to come too close that it would be less painful than loving and waiting for the undeniable escape.

In John 10:28-30, we find these Jesus Words that I just adore! He is just so gentle, so loving, so present! I think that if we truly began to know Him and His heart, it would so change the way that we view absolutely everything about our lives and our world!

In this passage, He tells us that the Father has placed the sheep (us) in the care of Jesus. No one can snatch us from the hand of the Father – the Hand of Christ.

When we are in Christ, we are safe.

We are loved.

We are protected.

We are cared for.

We are His.

His plan for us is good – not evil.

Every single thing that He orchestrates in our lives is for His glory and our benefit, even and especially when we don't understand.

In John 10:10, He tells us, "The thief comes to kill, steal, and destroy. But I come that you may have life and that you may have it in the abundance."

Too many times, we blame and accuse the Love-Giver, the Creator of our souls for our personal tragedies. We hold Him responsible for our unhappiness – for our failed plans and shattered dreams. Somewhere in the quiet place of our soul, we have attributed the Giver of Life with the character of the Taker of lives (the enemy.) Somewhere in the place of chaos and grief, we forget that God is actually good. And that He genuinely, authentically loves us – even and especially in the beautiful, broken places of our lives.

Precious one, we are safe in His care.

He is not the daddy who left you with streaks across your face or bruises on your back. He is not the husband who mistreats you and shames you in public. He is not the son who has grown bigger and stronger than you, bullying you for giving boundaries. He is not the man who violates you, touching you in private places behind locked doors. He is not the one who broke your heart and cancelled the promises. He is not the one who puts you in harm's way or manipulates you for his own gain. He is not the one who orchestrated tragedy in your life or who ripped your family apart at the seams. He is not the one who left you in poverty or deprived of joy. He is none of these things. He is not like any of these people.

Yet, too many times, we do with God what I did with outsiders. We think that if we don't gather together with other believers (fellowship) or read His heart (Word) or talk to Him daily (prayer), that somehow we are protecting ourselves from immense pain. Because what if our mistakes are too bad? What if we have gone too far? What if we don't believe enough? What if we don't love enough? What if we can't see a way out of the mess that we have made? Then certainly... He will leave us too. Certainly, He will abandon His creation, just as family abandons family.

And this is exactly how the enemy (thief) captures our hearts and minds with fear. He lies, laced with enough truth and a dash of shame to make us eat from his hand. And then we fall prey to his scheme. Suddenly, our joy is depleted. Our faith is weakened. Our hope seems lost. Our lives become powerless. And as long as you and I stay in this place, continuing to eat the morsels of shame, defeat, and fear, the enemy wins for that day.

Beautiful girl, it is time to reclaim what the enemy has stolen. It is time to heal our minds and souls from the toxin of the enemy and be restored by the Giver of Life and Love.

In His hands, we are safe and protected! We must choose to trust Him – even as we are surrounded by fragments of our lives, pieces that we have no clue what to do with or what they even are. All He wants is our hearts and our trust. And He will do the rest. We simply must invite Him to do so.

"Remember not the former things, nor consider the things of old. Behold, I am doing a new thing: Now it springs forth, do you not perceive it? I will make a way in the wilderness and rivers in the desert." Isaiah 43:18-19

5:RIVERS IN THE DESERT

They were in their favorite place, their sacred place. The place where the peace of God always seems to surround them, refreshing their hearts and restoring their souls! It was their anniversary weekend, and they had come here to hide away from all of the chaos and all of the noise… all of the day to day responsibilities and the rushing of the world. They loved to come here to soak in the precious moments of sharing life and love together.

The weather was perfect! Exactly how they liked it. Blazing sun on their faces and the salty breath of the ocean's wind greeting them as they closed their eyes and felt their entire bodies relax with each crash of the waves.

It was their 6th anniversary, and their dream was so close to becoming a reality that they could literally taste it! Only 4 months before, they had received the most coveted piece of mail that prospective adoptive parents desire…. The Happy Mail! The letter that confirms after years of interviews, paperwork, essays, meetings and home visits, that they have been deemed eligible to become a parent!

Once this letter arrives, it's only a matter of time before decisions are made and babies are placed and families are formed! The hardest part was now complete: 4 years of waiting for the determination approval letter. Now, they simply had to wait…… for the call.

One of my precious friends is currently holding his place in the waiting line of life. And for those of us who are natural "do-ers," the type A, self-motived, driven, let's do it right now kind of people, the waiting line is the absolute most frustrating place to be.

It feels as if we are simply waiting for Nothing. For action to happen – that we have No control over whatsoever - and life is literally mocking us because no matter how much we want to do something, we have no authority to do anything at all.

At times, we may even begin to wonder if we have somehow gotten lost in the shuffle, if our ticket was misplaced, and we are just serving as a place-holder.

We know that there is a calling on our lives.

We know that He has specific and magnificent plans lined up for us and works to complete! Yet, for some reason, we end up in this place where we have just enough information to know the destination that we are headed and slow movement is happening towards that direction, but we just haven't been released to go full-force into that new territory. For the moment, we are living in this waiting space.

While we are itching to do something – anything – to feel productive… He tells us to be patient, to wait. We have all of these ideas! We can create agendas, raise funds, inform others, write things, make plans… but again, He calls us to be patient. To wait. Be still. Trust. Trust. Trust.

It goes against literally everything ingrained within our core to be still and to wait. Yet, this is the very thing that we are called to do. Because we are not actively checking off our master task list, we mistakenly assume that we are not making any progress at all. Because we are not "working," we reject the idea that anything productive is actually taking root and creating momentum towards the dream.

It's like instructing a demanding 2 year old to be patient while you shop at Wal-Mart – and you've already been there for over 45 minutes.

Wait.

And for many of us – myself included – the response often resembles that of the toddler. Complete meltdown. Pass the wine, please.

Yet, as we attempt to rush the Creator of Life and Love or to move ahead of Him out of spite, we risk people getting hurt. We risk opportunities being missed. We risk the beautiful and profound moments that are birthed out of the mundane. The moments that we discount as inconsequential are many times the very moments where the weeds are being cut down to reveal the path in the wilderness. And if we rush by too quickly or run ahead of Him before the path has been cleared, we are at risk for missing the beauty that He is so graciously designing out of the broken. The masterpiece made from the remnants of tragedy. The hope glimmer that is given only after the darkest night.

Our God is always working and moving on our behalf for our good, and He is a Master at intertwining lives and story lines so that multiple families are benefactors of His goodness and glory through the same thread. Yet, too many times we fall prey to the lie that He isn't working or moving because we don't see the evidence. We become defeated by this false assumption because we fail to pause and reflect on His goodness.

I don't believe that it is by coincidence that He continuously calls us to Remember Him. In Deuteronomy 8:11-16, we are given these words:

"Take care lest you forget the Lord your God by not keeping his commandments and his rules and his statues, which I command you today, lest when you have eaten and are full and have built good houses and live in them, and when your herds and flocks multiply and your silver and gold is multiplied and all that you have is multiplied, then your heart be lifted up, and you forget the Lord your God, who brought you out of the land of Egypt, out of the house of slavery, who led you through the great and terrifying wilderness with its fiery serpents and scorpions and thirsty ground where there was no water, who brought you water out of the flinty rock, who fed you in the wilderness with manna that your fathers did not know, that he might humble you and test you, to do you good in the end."

We must Remember where He has been with us, what He has led us through and how He has provided so that in these moments where we are standing in the waiting line of life, waiting for movement that we cannot generate or sifting through shattered pieces of our lives left from tragedies unexpected, that here… in these moments… we have engraved within our very hearts and minds, the mark of Jesus. Love-letters written to us. His Word. The places where He has graced us with His Love and delivered us from our gut-wrenching sorrow. Memories that we have so carefully stored and packaged for times such as these.

Like an empty-nester mom who retrieves her collection of photos to relive those moments once again, so we must return to our Creator of Life and pause to Remember Him. For it is in this place of remembrance where we find our lungs releasing fear and inhaling trust. It is here, in this place of remembrance where we remember the curtain being drawn back – so that we could see a glimpse of how He was working in our lives, when we didn't even have a clue of what He was doing or how He was transforming lives. It is here – in the Remembrance – where our hope and faith is restored.

There is a danger when we fail to stop remembering. We begin to think that we can do it all ourselves. We fail to surrender our hearts and instead, we choose to pick up weapons for self-preservation. We resort to becoming our own god, choosing our own way, defining our own future – rather than resting and trusting in Him and His Sovereignty.

In Hebrews 11:1, we are given the picture of faith. "Now faith is the assurance of things hoped for, the conviction of things not seen."

Faith chooses trust. Faith chooses to place belief and trust in the Creator of Love before the evidence of what it actually sees. And as we practice the gift of Remembrance, trust becomes easier because we are able to track the footprints of Love showing up in the most vulnerable places and restoring what we once believed was lost. Like most things in life, it's much easier to capture the evidence of miracles when you are watching from the rear-view mirror rather than in the whirlwind of chaos.

Faith chooses to rest in the certainty of knowing that God is good, and His plans are always working in our favor. When we come to truly know the Lover of our souls, we are no longer chained to the soul-sucking, rule-following, not-enoughness that religion generates. Following religion is absolutely exhausting. I know, I have done it for quite some time – and almost completely drowned in the pew, sitting among wolves disguised as sheep.

When we come to truly meet and know Jesus – not the one of religion – but the one who would rather leave the deacon's meeting to go and have dinner with friends, the one who would rather wait for hours for a woman that he is not supposed to even talk to in public, to bring healing to her heart – rather than to go and do religious things, the one who shows up when community leaders and religious authority have stones in hand and ready to murder the adulteress based on the law of the land…. And He chooses to offer Grace…

When we come to know this One, we come to know the God of Love. The God who delights in gracing His people - not condemning them. "For God so Loved the world that he gave his Only Son, that whoever believes in him should not perish but have eternal life. For God did not send his Son into the world to condemn the world, but in order that the world might be saved through him." John 3:16-17

His heart has never been to cast people out, to reject, to harm, or to hurt. Everything that He has ever done and ever will do will always be founded on the premise of Love and Grace. He provided the way out – so that we could find redemption through Him, His Name, His Blood, His sacrifice. And as we come to know this Jesus – the One of Love and mercy and compassion, our hearts find it easier to trust and rest in Him – knowing that He is truly good.

To know that we can trust Him in the midst of our most vulnerable places, in our worst fears, in our failed hopes is to give the Author and Finisher of our faith the keys to our lives to work miracles. To restore the shattered pieces. To heal the wounds. To bring beauty out of the ashes of our lives.

Maybe you are also one of the ones in the waiting line of life. Maybe you are waiting for the promised promotion or for the answer to a prayer that you have been requesting for years. Maybe you are waiting for that phone call – the one that will change everything about your life. Whatever it is that you are waiting for, know that He is in the midst. He is working behind the scenes, speaking to hearts, preparing circumstances, preparing the way. He is doing things that you and I cannot even begin to perceive – much less understand.

And while we are not given a Disney Land "Fast Pass" to skip through the line and to eliminate the frustration of forced patience, He is calling us to enter into a space that moves us from self-reliance to faith-surrender.

On the day my parents were celebrating their 6th anniversary and enjoying the fullness of their life waiting room – located at the beach – I was being born. Little did they know that at the exact hour that they sat, dipping their toes into the hot sand and wondering aloud if their baby had been born, I was sucking in my first breaths of air and crying my first tears.

Before I had ever been removed by the hands of a stranger and claimed an orphan by the state of NC, the Lord had already prepared for me – a home, a family, and a new name.

And the Giver of Grace, the Restorer of Broken Dreams does everything He orchestrates with complete Love and perfection! He chose to write our story by giving me a birth date on the same exact day as my parent's anniversary.

Beautiful one, so many times we are pushing ourselves to recreate our lives, to rewrite our stories, to improve ourselves so that we can be whole.

Yet, what He is calling us to do is to come before Him with a raw, surrendered heart and lay down all of our self-preservation tools at His feet. He is inviting us to come and simply be still. To soak in His presence. To trust in His plan – and even more, to trust in Him.

There is a new, glorious thing that He is doing. He is indeed, making a way out of no way, bringing forth running waters in the desert of our parched lives. He is picking up all of the broken fragments of our damaged lives, and He is breathing grace, hope, and restoration into every shattered piece.

And while He holds our hearts and lives in the palm of His Almighty Hand, bringing order to chaos and beauty out of ashes, He calls us to do the most important thing of all:"Be still and know that I am God." Psalm 46:10

"For I know the plans that I have for you, declares the Lord, plans for welfare and not for evil, to give you a future and a hope."
Jeremiah 29:11

6: REMEMBERING HIS GOODNESS

They were working at their store, Sportsman's World in Elizabeth City, NC, when they received the collect call. It was September 2, 1980 when they learned that in that very instant, their lives had completely changed! Every prayed that they had prayed... every interview that they had completed... every document that they had signed had all come down to this... this very moment. The day that they learned that they had a daughter – a baby girl – waiting for them to come and take her home!

It would only be a few days before they would travel to Greensboro, NC and meet their precious one, their long-awaited child. Finally, they would have the family that they had so dreamed of becoming!

Yet, as I write these words of this happy ending of dreams restored, I am well aware of how many of you are silently struggling with situations, lives that seem to be at a complete dead-end.

Six months ago, a friend of mine from high-school encountered some health issues and frantically left work to find relief, and hopefully answers for her discomfort. Little did she know that when she left for the Emergency Room on that summer day, that she would never again return home. Never again would she hold her 2 year old baby girl or text her mother goodnight. In one weekend, this entire family would change forever as Melissa breathed her last breath and left this world for another.

Now, her mother is raising her beautiful daughter and struggling daily to understand why the Creator of Life and Love would allow this tragedy in their lives. Holidays are met with an empty space at the table, and sadness absorbs her heart. So many questions are left unanswered, and deep in her soul, she wonders how healing can ever be found.

On July 3, 2017, one of my dearest friends and sister of heart received the call that every mother fears. Her precious baby boy, Isaiah was tragically taken by the hands of a killer while leaving a late night house party.

A random drive-by shooting stole the breath and life of her precious son. Never again would she have the opportunity to hold his hand, to hold him close, to look deep into his eyes and tell him how much he is loved. Through this hostile act of evil, a man-child was murdered and this family was ripped apart at the seams.

This was the second child that she has lost in this world. The first was Benjamin, a remarkable young man with a faith in God bigger than most can even comprehend. Diagnosed with retinoblastoma, Ben was forced to learn how to navigate life without the gift of sight. Yet, choosing to embrace his abilities rather than his limitations, he transformed the world through his love and passion for life!

At the age of 17, precious Ben lost his battle with his cancer, but celebrated the final moments of his life because he knew that he was a child of God! Not only did this 17 year old kid have no fear, he rejoiced in the truth of knowing that he was going home to the Giver of Love, the Creator of Life! His deepest passion was making certain that others would have this same peace in their own lives.

When you speak to their mother, Aquanetta Gordon and hear the heart of this warrior woman, she will smile in the midst of the pain and speak with bold faith wrapped in the voice of grace and love.

Only a few days after losing her Isaiah baby, I called her to see how she was doing, to offer my love – even though it felt so helpless. Yet, during this phone call, these were the words that this faith-filled woman shared, "Liz, I forgive him. I forgive the man who killed my baby. Because there is no way that he has any idea what he has actually done to me or to my family. How can I ask God to forgive me of my sins if I'm not willing to forgive him? I so wish that he could come to know the Jesus that I know and love and serve. Because this boy, this man... he needs to be redeemed. He needs to be restored. And I really hope that they can find the one who did this. Who is responsible. So I can go to him directly, look him in the eye, and let him know, that I forgive him."

I will never forget that conversation and the impact that it had on my heart. This was from the heart of a mother who had just learned a few days prior that her baby was dead. Killed by the murderous hands of another man. And she was able to already find the place of grace and love and forgiveness.

This is what Jesus does. This is how His Spirit works. And when we live in the place of Remembrance – always holding tight to the truth of who the Giver of Love is and how He has delivered us from our own bondage – it's easier to trust Him in the pain, the brokenness, the tragedy.

There isn't a day that passes that this precious friend of mine does not desperately miss her son and wish that she could touch him again. Yet, because she has come to know and trust the Lord with all of her heart and with all of her soul, she knows that He is still at work for the good – even when the suffering is immeasurable.

Isaiah 55:8-9 declares, "For my thoughts are not your thoughts, neither are your ways my ways, declares the Lord. For as the Heavens are higher than the earth, so are my ways higher than your ways and my thoughts higher than your thoughts."

There will be places of brokenness in our lives that we simply cannot control, fix or resolve. For some, it may be the unanswered prayer for children or the tragic murder of a child. It may be the diagnosis that you were not expecting and changes everything or the child who is locked behind prison doors for poor mistakes and selfish choices. It may be the loved one who battles drug addiction, and they cannot seem to conquer the war. It may be the one who battles severe mental illness and finds themselves living as a ward of the state.

The fragments of brokenness run wide and deep – and no one is immune. No family can escape. No amount of money can deter it from entering your home and life. Brokenness reaches across homes in every social circle and every ethnicity. There is simply no discrimination in the places that evil preys and tragedy strikes.

Yet, the Giver of Grace did not create us to remain shackled in a place of pity and shame. We were not designed to remain broken. It is His heart and has always been His plan to bring redemption to broken lives, restoration to shattered dreams, and to buy us back from the hand of the enemy. Since the creation of the world, there has been a plan in place to make us whole…. Even when it would cost the Giver of Love and Life everything, including Himself.

"If you abide in My Word, you are truly My disciples, and you will know the truth, and the truth will set you free." John 8:31-32

7: CREATED BY LOVE – FOR A PURPOSE AND WITH A PURPOSE.

I absolutely love the meme that is quite popular right now that states, "I'm not your ride or die chik. I've got questions like... where are we going? How long are we staying? Who will be there? Can we get food on the way?" I could see this at least a hundred times and giggle every single time. Because this is so me!

I do have questions, and I have a lot of them, all of the time about all of the things. And I have been this way for as far back as I can possibly remember. Yet, many of the questions that I have housed in my heart for decade upon decade were ones that no one could actually answer.

Questions like: Do I look like my biological mom or dad? What did my dad think of me? Did he even care that they gave me away? What about his other girls, and his wife? Did they know about me? What are they like? Did she give me a birth name? If so, what was it? Where was I actually born? What did she look like? Are there any pictures of me at birth? What was I like when I finally got to the foster home, and who were they? Did they have other children? Did she stay at home with me, or was I in daycare during that time? Have any of them even thought about me since they gave me away or have they forgotten?

In 1980, when you are placed for adoption through Children's Home Society, your complete identity becomes confiscated, sealed, and altered – immediately. I am convinced that the FBI has taken notes from this agency on how to preserve confidentiality!

31

Once you have been given your new family, all of the details of your former life, such as name, place of birth, parents' names and addresses are edited to match that of the new family. Everything that was actually true about your actual birth and real identity during the moments that you gulped your first breaths of air and ran salty tears down your cheeks are completely deleted and locked away by government officials who make their career standing guard over this vault of sealed data to ensure that we never gain access to our own information, to our own identity.

My thirsty quest for answers about my identity has no reflection at all on the performance of my parents' parenting skills and nurture capacity. They have loved me fiercely since day one and have always strived diligently to protect me at all costs from the dangers of the world, and most often – from myself.

The questions that I battled – the answers that I was seeking had nothing to do with insufficient family, but rather a deeply rooted need to know the truth of my identity. As I struggled to find my place in this world, I found that my greatest challenge was not the circumstances that surrounded me, but rather, the war that raged within my own heart.

Because I did not have answers, I filled in the blanks with self-sabotaging beliefs, the morsels of the enemy. Because I had no evidence that my biological parents were concerned about my where-abouts, I concluded that they could care less. Because I had never seen a picture of me at birth, I determined that I was not valuable enough to have new born photos of myself. And each time that the Father of Lies, the Master of Manipulation offered me a morsel of self-hate, I would willingly take it from his hand. Because I had recited and rehearsed these lies for so long, I had come to believe them as truth.

Years ago, I remember a sermon that was taught about the power of truth and authenticity. Pastor Bob Copeland explained that new bank associates were trained to identify counterfeit bills. He shared that they would spend hour upon hour, day upon day working with authentic bills. They learned what it looks like, feels like, and even how it smells. They would invest so many hours engaging with the authentic, that when a counterfeit would attempt to make its way into their hands, they would immediately recognize its falsehood.

The Lover of our Souls is literally obsessed with Truth. It resonates in everything that He touches and in absolutely every work that He delivers. He understands the gift and power of truth in our lives and the danger that lurks in the shadows when we choose to dismiss the authentic for the artificial.

In John 14:6, God-with-Us gives us these powerful words, "I am the Way, the Truth, and the Life. No man comes to the Father, except through Me." Our God is so incredibly passionate about loving us, inviting us, welcoming us, and embracing us that He simply could not allow His children to not receive the invitation to the ultimate party!

He's like the popular kid who is having the Best House Party ever – and everyone (literally, everyone) is invited! You just have to have the right code at the door to be welcomed in the door!

Jesus is the code. He is the password. And He is exposing the Truth for all to see so that no one is left out of all this glorious fun!

It has been over 30 years of wondering, questioning about parts of my life, my identity. Some of the questions have been answered, while others remain in the mystery box of my life.

Yet, what the Grace-Giver has been teaching me throughout this journey is that my identity is not based on the beginnings of my life. My identity is not based on where I was born or who was responsible for my genetics. My value is not dependent upon baby pictures taken or how many times I have been thought about from another person.

All of these things are part of my story and have led me to the place where I am today, at this very moment. However, none of these things determine my value or worth. My identity is based on Jesus, and that I belong to Him. My identity is based on the Giver of Hope, the Restorer of Souls and the Way, the Truth, and the Life. He is the One whom I should be thirsting for daily.

For He is the Only One who can offer me peace in the chaos, joy in the sufferings, and wisdom for the days ahead. Knowing my past and humble beginnings will not lend fulfillment for this day and hope for the future. But knowing the authentic love, grace, and mercy of the One who is Truth provides my soul with the sustenance I that need to sustain everyday life.

In Philippians 4:8, He shares the secret for silencing the voices that we want so desperately to bury, the insecurities that keep us lying awake at night in distress. He gives us these words, these instructions:

"Finally brothers, whatever is true, whatever is honorable, whatever is just, whatever is pure, whatever is lovely, whatever is commendable, if there is any excellence, or if there is anything worthy of praise, think about these things."

Precious girl, this is the list that leads to powerful thoughts and sabotages the plans of evil regarding our minds. Because He knows that our thoughts are such a powerful force in our everyday lives, He gives us a standard of which to measure against to ensure that we are positioning our minds towards the Giver of Grace and Love rather than the Father of Lies and the Ultimate Condemner and Shamer of Souls.

What are the voices of shame that you need to silence? What are the words of inadequacy, unworthiness that you need to bury indefinitely? What are the fears that have held you captive or the regrets that call you by name? Whatever these are for you, it's time to break free. It's time to reclaim the promises of your Life-Giver, your Hope-Maker, your Soul-Deliverer.

Beautiful one, if you were sitting across from me right now, I would offer you some delicious coffee…. And then ask you to close your eyes and soak in these words of truth…

You are not your past mistakes.

You are not the things that have happened to you.

You are not a mistake.

Your identity is not found or formed or based on man.

Your story is not irredeemable.

You have been created by Love – for a purpose and with a purpose. You simply must allow your story to be rebirthed, repurposed, restored.

But here is the thing…. We cannot chase after grace while we coddle lies. We cannot seek healing and restoration if we refuse to surrender our deepest wounds. We cannot find truth if we are unwilling to invest in the Authentic.

To find true healing for our hearts and redemption for our souls… to find deliverance from the pain and an identity that is wrapped in grace rather than calculated by performance… we must be willing to allow the Giver of Truth access into our souls so that evil lies can be exposed. Wounds can be healed and truth poured in. The place where beauty from ashes can truly begin…

But it all must begin with the Truth, the Great I Am!

"Everyone who drinks of this water will be thirsty again, but whoever drinks of the water that I will give him will become in him a spring of water welling up to eternal life." John 4:13-14

8: BEAUTY OF THE BROKENNESS

It was the hottest part of the day when she arrived at the well. She was thirsty and needed to draw water. Yet, while others had come earlier in the morning to avoid the heat, she had deliberately waited until noon to avoid them.

The women. The ones who mocked her behind closed doors and who shamed her by their hostile looks and nasty gestures. Many of them spent their time in religious circles, but it was evident that they hated her.

Her life was much different than theirs.

She hadn't intended for it to become this way. It's just how it had played out. Poor choices, lack of trust, failed promises, unrealistic expectations – all of these things had weaved its way into her life, into her home, into her relationships.

They knew nothing of these things and the sorrow that she lived with each day. They just judged her, declaring marks of shame upon her and her life – every single time they had the opportunity to do so. It seemed that they had created a new form of entertainment for themselves in rejecting her. For every time that they branded her with another mark of disdain, they elevated their personal standing in the invisible field of comparison.

She had learned that they she could not bend their opinions or generate any favor in their eyes, so she did the only thing that she knew to do to preserve the remnants of her heart – avoid them, at all costs.

When she arrived at the well, there was a man there. He was all alone and didn't even have a cup to fill with water. Yet, the interesting thing is that he didn't seem to be in a hurry to leave. It was the strangest thing, but she chose to not question. She had certainly had her share of criticism from strangers for misunderstanding her life and circumstances; the very last thing that she wanted was to offer this same judgment to others.

Yet, when He spoke to her, asking for a cup of water, she could not hide the element of surprise! For in their culture, it was completely taboo for a man to speak to a woman in public – especially a stranger! Not only this, but He was a Jew. She was a Samaritan, and everyone knew that this was a line to never be crossed. The culture had deemed her ineligible, unworthy of even being acknowledged due to her genetic disposition and the color of her skin. For all of these reasons, she could not even begin to fathom how and why He would choose to speak to her.

With a facial expressions that held no secrets, she knew that she had to respond. Certainly, He had already calculated all of her questions by the look on her face! And when she questioned Him about His behavior, He simply smiled at her and offered these words, "If you knew the gift of God and who it is that is saying to you, 'Give me a drink,' you would have asked him, and he would have given you living water."

This precious woman is standing before Giver of Life, the Lover of our souls – and yet, she has no idea that it is even Him!

He has come here – in this moment, at this very place – to bring healing to her deepest wounds and redeem years lost. While others mock and shame her, He waits patiently for her arrival – so that she can truly know that she is loved. She is wanted. She is precious. She is treasured. She is valuable. She is enough. Exactly as she is…. Even and especially, in the midst of all of her brokenness.

How I absolutely adore the Lover of our Souls!

Beloved one, so many times, we have this false notion that we cannot come and be with Jesus until we have all of our lives in order and all of the broken pieces are out of sight.

Yet, what we fail to realize is that when we are hiding from the world, positioning ourselves so that we can avoid the unwanted conversations and the uninvited judgment from others, we have a Grace-Giver who is patiently waiting for us, to pour into us, and to offer His gift of life…. Eternal life.

How many times have I attempted to fill my own vessel with other things to somehow prove my worth and proclaim my identity? How many groups have I joined or meetings have I attended in a vain attempt to confirm that my life holds value? How many times have I avoided the people who sit in pews with the law of legalism in their hands because I had a broken life that I was unable to fix – and could no longer bear the weight of their hostile rejection? How many nights have I sobbed myself to sleep, praying to the God of my childhood that somehow my life would count and my breath would hold meaning for others?

And here, He waits.

With grace in one hand. And love poured out in the other.

With battle scars embedded in His hands where the cold, rusty nails were driven through His flesh to proclaim innocence for the guilty and life for the walking dead. Where blood gushed from His body so that broken people could be restored.

While others judge, shame, mock, and wage war with words of hate and self-righteous deeds, the Way of Peace greets us in the brokenness and proclaims, "Everyone who drinks of this water will be thirsty again, but whoever drinks of the water that I will give him will never be thirsty again. The water that I will give him will become in him a spring of water welling up to eternal life." John 4:13-14

He did not exclude her because she had a poor track record with men and marriage. He was fully aware that her past included 5 husbands and a current man in the picture whom she was not yet married to.

He knew her story.

And He chose her anyway.

Beloved one, don't miss this! He knew her story. And He chose her anyway!

Her brokenness did not disqualify her from the gift of grace and love. If anything, it was a prerequisite! For how can we truly be restored and healed if we fail to acknowledge that we are broken? How can we receive Living water if we refuse to admit that we are even thirsty?

The beauty of brokenness is the power that rests in its limitations, weaknesses and vulnerability. For when we are weak, He is strong. When we are at the end of ourselves and cannot find a way to calm the storm, we are in the perfect position for the Grace-Giver to do His best work!

With hands surrendered, hearts poured out and knees bent towards the Maker of the Stars, we relinquish our pride, our tools for self-preservation, and our flawed best efforts so that the Redemption-Giver can breathe His breath on all of the broken pieces of our lives....

And create Beauty from Ashes.

"Love is patient and kind; love does not envy or boast; it is not arrogant or rude. It does not insist on its own way; it is not irritable or resentful; it does not rejoice at wrongdoing, but rejoices with the truth. Love bears all things, believes all things, hopes all things, endures all things." 1 Corinthians 13:4-7

9: WHERE AUTHENTIC LOVE EXISTS.

I was sixteen years old when he showed up unexpected at our home. My parents were still at work, and my brother was somewhere in the neighborhood playing with friends.

He was a U.S. Marine, and I was a junior in high school. We had been together throughout my high school career, and in my limited understanding of relationships and love, I sincerely believed that this was it.

He was four years older than me and had enlisted in the Marine Corps upon graduation. So the concept of experiencing a normal dating relationship was completely obsolete. Our connection primarily existed through the writing of letters, brief phone calls, and on occasion, time together when he was on leave.

Appearance was everything to him. Not only did he make it his personal goal to serve as the center of attention at all costs, he also wanted me to follow suit.

On days that he was on leave, he would instruct me which outfits he preferred for me to wear, how to fix my hair, and what shade of lipstick he liked best. I learned to check my own opinion at the door and table my own thoughts to appease him.

Although I had no interest in joining the military myself, he would pass down his training material for me to read. He wanted me to not only recognize the various ranks, but to be able to address each person properly.

I was expected to know the jargon, to understand the code, to recognize the bars of honor. And while he was off at training, he expected me to be on "my best behavior" and make certain that I was following suit.

It didn't matter how many miles were between us, he found a way to confirm my fidelity. Once he called from Puerto Rico to share with me that had had people watching me, to make sure that I was representing him well.

He then began to affirm the outfit that I had worn to school that day, people that I had spoken with and essentially, specific details from that day. And these were the days when the only phone that was available was your landline. Facebook was not even a thing.

My parents knew of none of this.

As an angry teen who questioned her value, self - worth, and purpose of existence, I had come to believe that he was what I actually deserved.

In his eyes, I was nothing more than a possession – a girl to hold on his arm while wearing his Dress Blues and then offering me to his best friend as his date to his senior prom when he didn't have one. He even added that personal benefits were attached to the deal since he was his best friend.

Thankfully, his friend chose to only accept the prom date piece and never requested anything more.

For four years, I was trained to take orders, to not question, to hold no opinions, and to make him look good – at all costs.

By my Junior year, I noticed that his letters began to change. The content began to darken, and he had become consumed with the idea that I was cheating on him.

This was simply not true, but he was convinced it was.

The phone calls began to increase, and I was not home at the exact moment that he expected me to be, he always assumed that I was with someone else.

At sixteen years old, I had learned the fear of having another person, a supposed loved one attempt to control your life. And I had no idea how to make it stop.

I was not expecting the knock on the door, to see him there at my home. There was this look in his eye that I will never forget – this sick thrill of breaking laws and creating fears.

He asked me to come out to his car; he had something to show me. And as he popped the trunk, he exploded with excitement at his new toys! Explosive ones. Stolen ones. Ones that had removed without permission from the military base and placed in his personal car. Now sitting in our drive way.

He had taken an M16 and a live hand grenade from the base and was driving around with it in his personal car like it was a Nerf gun.

And as he looked at my face and saw the color drain away, my heart pounding with fear, he stared deep into my eyes and breathed these words, "If you ever cheat on me, I will come to your house like I did today. And I will kill your mom, dad and brother – and make you watch. And then I will kill you. And then I will kill myself."

With those chilling words, he closed his trunk, returned to his car and drove away.

And with my every breath, I believed him.

I was one of the incredibly fortunate ones. I had no idea how to get out of this. My parents didn't even have any idea that I was in this. And I was embarrassed beyond description that I had allowed myself to fall into this place. This trap. And the thing that confused me even more was the fact that I loved him in spite of it. And somehow in the midst of all of the fear, the appearance factor, the intimidation and the threats, I sincerely believed that he loved me too.

He would soon receive orders to serve in Puerto Rico, and this would ultimately, lead to my freedom. Soon, he would fall in love with a woman there, cheat on me, and end our relationship to pursue a life with her. The life that I had become accustomed to would fall away, and I would be given the grace gift of a new beginning, a new day.

Embedded deep within our hearts and souls is a space created by Love – for Love. We are created for relationship with the Divine Giver of Life, and we are pieced together with the Master intent to love one another. Our entire lives are orchestrated by the Creator with these two forces in play!

He is so passionate about this Love-Agenda that when cornered by a lawyer and questioned about His teachings and the priority of His commandments, He gave us these very words:

"You shall love the Lord your God with all your heart and with all your soul and with all your mind. This is the great and first commandment. And a second is like it: You shall love your neighbor as yourself. On these two commandments depend all the Law and the Prophets." Matthew 22:37-40

Yet, too many times, we fail to allow Him, the Lover of our Souls to meet us in the space that He created for love. We attempt to fill our own cups, to satisfy our own thirst through the love and acceptance of others. We invite the counterfeit into our lives and establish relationships which cause immense pain and confusion. Because we have neglected to invest in the Authentic love, we do not even realize that we have been entertaining the artificial.

The Love-Designer did not create this gift to be misused, abused, and manipulated. Love was not created to be a bargaining tool or a device to control another. The Love-Gift that we are created and designed for is one of beauty, sacrifice, and service. It is a representation of the Love Gift, the Grace Giver who gave Himself to bring us into His safe care.

In 1 Corinthians 13, He offers to us these words, this glorious depiction of how authentic love actually lives and gives itself to others:

"Love is patient and kind; love does not envy or boast, it is not arrogant or rude. It does not insist on its own way; it is not irritable or resentful. It does not rejoice at wrong doing, but rather rejoices with the truth. Love bears all things, hopes all things, endures all things. Love never ends."

As we choose to engage the Authentic, to learn from the true Love-Giver and to delight in the wholeness of His love, we find that our souls are simply not content with the counterfeit. We will no longer position ourselves to be property or place holders or a place for unwarranted anger to be released.

Our souls are thirsty for more – and it is a thirst that can only be quenched with genuine, unconditional love. The love that can only come from the Living Water.

Precious one, I invite you to a place where you are safe from harm. A place where you are safe from judgment. I invite you to a space where love opens its arms and welcomes you in. A place where your heart can find rest and be restored. A place where rejection and hatred are not allowed to enter. I invite you to a place where you are loved. You are treasured. You are valued. You are heard. I invite you to a place where you are respected and also adored. I invite you to the threshold of Grace, to the Giver of Love, to the One who is waiting patiently to bind up your broken heart and to heal your deepest wounds. I invite you to the One who knows your heart and has your name inscribed in the palm of His hands. I invite you to your Comforter, your Peace, your Wisdom, your Strength. I invite you the Restorer of Souls and the Redeemer of Life... the Great I Am!

I invite you to come with all of your fragments and broken pieces – your failed dreams – your aborted hopes – your locked up memories and scars of abuse. I invite you to come with all of the voices that you cannot silence, with all of the questions that you cannot answer and all of the hot mess that you cannot fix. I invite you to come with all of your insecurities and doubts – your fears and your flooding hot tears. I invite you to come to the One who waits by the well – to meet you here – in the hottest hour of the day, when all you want is to simply disappear.

I invite you to come and drink from this cup.

Taste this Living water.

Drink and be filled.

He is here to offer you the life that you dream of and cannot afford. A life of peace and joy. A life of soul fire and comfort and rest. It is here in this place that He waits for you to choose and drink.... To choose to become well.

Because healing can only be given for those who truly desire to be made well. And beauty can only arise from ashes that are willingly released.

I invite you to come and be made well.

Drink from the Living water and place all of the broken pieces at His feet.

Come and be made well as He redeems you from your sorrow and breathes life into your soul. And all of the broken fragments of your life will now be made whole.

A Beautiful new creation that only He can design when we surrender our ashes for His beauty, Divine.

I invite you to come to the well.

"There is therefore now no condemnation for those who are in Christ Jesus. For the law of the Spirit of life has set you free in Christ Jesus from the law of sin and death."
Romans 8:1-2

10: WHEN GRACE SHOWS UP

She will never forget the moment that she met Him.

She had seen Him throughout the village and had heard the rumors about the miracles. She just didn't know what to make of any of it.

He was unlike anyone that they had ever encountered before.

He was teaching in the Synagogue, and it appeared that He was quite popular. There was always a mob of people following Him wherever He went, hoping that they might capture the next miracle event or His most current teaching.

But she had also learned that there was a group of people who resented Him with every fiber of their being. She didn't understand it – because most of them were religious leaders. The ones who knew the Law of Moses and could recite it word for word.

Yet, something about this Man, this Miracle-Maker greatly intimidated them… creating fear and distrust among these religious people.

He seemed to be a Man of Peace – with no hostile agenda attached, but who was she to really know?

If truth be told, religion just wasn't her thing.

It worked for many, and she respected that. But for her personally – it just had too many rules. Way too many guidelines. She could barely even manage her own life. There was absolutely no way that she could have the energy to learn all of the do's and don'ts of this Sacred Script.

How do people even do this whole thing?

Her life was a complete mess – and she never intended for it to be this way. Although she wasn't a religious person, she did want to be a good person, a kind person, a loving person. And she tried.

47

But she made so many mistakes. She knew this about herself, which was another reason she added to her list of why she would never make it as a good synagogue girl!

There was this man that had held her attention captive for quite some time. She knew that he was married, but it was obvious that the marriage was not anything that brought him any happiness or joy. She didn't mean to end up in this place. Really, she didn't. Somehow, it just seemed to happen.

Looks that lingered just a moment too long... conversations that connected one to the other... and suddenly, she had become the very woman that she had secretly vowed to never become – an adulteress.

This was not the first time that they had engaged, but it was the only time that they had ever been caught. It was the most humiliating day of her life. All of her shame was exposed for everyone to see.

She wasn't even sure how they knew or how they found them. But they did.

She was barely dressed when they arrived – the religious people – to come and violently force her from the home.

Their words were so hateful. All she could do was look at the ground. Tears rushed forward; she could not stop them. She didn't mean to end up in this place. She just wanted so desperately to be loved. And for the first time since she could even remember, this was what she felt like with him. Loved.

But she didn't want to hurt anyone in the process. And this was certainly how she wanted to be exposed. God, what had she done?

She didn't know where they were taking her or what would even happen. Yet, suddenly, they stopped abruptly – at the Synagogue.

This man. The one that she had heard about was teaching. There were people absolutely everywhere. And all of this was interrupted... for her. She was half clothed, half naked... with every bit of her shameful soul exposes for everyone to see.

Through rushing tears, she noticed their hands.

Along the way, they had picked up the largest stones that they could possibly find and were rolling them in their hands. She could smell the scent of murder, the breath of revenge. Like savage beasts, they were beyond ready to shatter her bones and pour out her blood. Simply because she had fallen in love with the wrong man. She had broken their rules.

This Teacher-Man was quiet. He, too, noticed their stones. But He waited to speak. He gently looked at her, locking eyes – and then glanced back at them – as they began to speak, declaring her guilt.

"Teacher," they said, "This woman has been caught in the act of adultery. Now in the Law, Moses commanded us to stone such women. So what do you say?"

It was all a set up. A ploy to take Him down.

The Teacher-Man who seemed to ruin their reputation, their fame, their power – because where they offered laws and rules and fear…. He offered freedom, love, and grace. His agenda made theirs obsolete. They worked to earn their righteousness. He was righteousness – calling His people to stop chasing after rules and rather, to follow after Him.

For He was the God gift in flesh seeking friends, family, community – not desiring slaves.

It was an intentional trap to find flaws in His teachings and to destroy His power. It just so happened that she was used as a token piece in this sick game.

She waited to hear the words that He would speak.

She knew that she was guilty. How could she even tell Him that she didn't mean to end up here? Like this? If only there was a way that He could know the secret places of her heart… the deepest wounds… the scars of rejection… the voices of insecurity that would not stop. If only He knew her past – the places that she had been – and how more than anything, she just wanted to matter. To someone. To anyone. And for whatever reason, it ended up being him.

Moments had passed and no words have even been uttered. They, too, were waiting. Hungry to strike. But this Man-Teacher said nothing as He thoughtfully bent down and began to write in the sand.

It felt like hours had passed, but really, it had only been moments. He wrote gently, patiently – with Love pouring from His eyes. He made certain that He looked at each of them individually – deep within their core – as His finger write words in the sand that simply halted their course.

He stood briefly to make the last remark, "Let him who is without sin among you, be the first to throw a stone at her." And He bent down once more, writing words with His finger in the sand.

She felt her breath come back when the first stone was dropped. There was an echo of defeat, a plan thwarted as stones fell and the angry mob of men began to walk away. One by one – the oldest ones first – until suddenly, she glanced up to find that none of her accusers were left.

This Teacher-Man stood up and looked at her – in all of her brokenness – in all of her shame. With love in His heart and grace in His hand, he asked, "Woman, where are they? Has no one condemned you?"

"No one, Lord," she replied. Tears streamed down her face. She deserved none of this forgiveness. Who was this Man?

The Soul-Redeemer smiled and gently replied, "Neither do I condemn you; go and from now on, sin no more." (John 8:1-11)

Beloved one, this is the One whom I have waited to introduce you to…. The One who was waiting for the woman at the well! The One who has created our lives, planned our births, and redeemed us from the pit! He is the Love-Creator, the Grace-Giver, the Soul Redeemer! And the grace gift that was offered to this precious daughter that we meet in John 8 is the same grace gift that He offers to us.

Some of us are in a place of being exposed at this very moment. Mistakes were made. Hearts were hurt. Lives were damaged. And we find ourselves confronted by workers of religion who seek to shatter our reputations and bleed out our names.

Others of us are in a place of hiding – deeply afraid of being exposed. We have found ourselves in a life that we have created.

We just didn't quite mean to end up here. And now, we are desperately trying to resolve it, restore it before it's too late.

There may be some of us who are part of the religious tribe. We have been taught that being good girls, following all of the rules, not straying from the Scribe will make us righteous. Because we have worked so diligently, so tirelessly to be this good religious girl, we secretly despise the girls who make us look really bad. The ones who break all the rules and then come in the back door expecting grace. The girls who do not play by any of the rules that we live by and yet they claim to like the Man-God-Teacher.

So we wait for them with stones in our hands. Only our stones are not tangible rocks from the ground. No, our stones are much different – but just as dangerous. They are our haughty words, our nasty attitudes and actions, our hateful stares. We pretend to be nice to their faces (sometimes), but we are secretly waiting for an opportunity to expose them. To catch them half naked and vulnerable - so that we can throw them before the religious leaders.

Some of us have heard of this Man-Teacher, but we aren't yet certain that He is trustworthy or has our best interest at heart. We are silently waiting in the corner, watching to see what this Man-Teacher has in store for our lives.

Whatever the place that you find yourself in… rather you are the half-naked chic exposed and shamed or the one clutching stones of judgment to shatter bones, you are both welcome here. In this place.

Because the truth is this….. we are all broken.

We are all truthfully exposed. It may not yet be viewed from the world, but it is certainly missed from the sight of Heaven.

Every single one of us have sinned, and none of us are righteous. It is only by the grace of Jesus that we are saved, and it is not by any works that we can do ourselves.

In the same place the adulteress is broken for breaking religious code and law of the land, falling in love with the wrong man…. The one who holds judgment in her heart and devises wicked schemes to justify her righteousness is just as guilty.

It's a heart issue that can only be healed by the Creator of hearts and the Giver of eternal life. He is calling us into a new place, into a new day where we choose to surrender our stones and to walk away from shame. He is inviting us to a life renewed where dreams are rebuilt and hopes are restored. Where the things of the former are put to rest and the life that we were created for is resurrected.

He is calling us into a new day, into a new creation where the broken pieces are mended – with enough small cracks still in place – so that the glimmer of His glory and grace can shine through. And the remnants of ashes will never be forgotten…. For they are the very foundation of this beautiful piece of art that He is uniquely creating…. A one of a kind masterpiece…. You.

"I will never leave you nor forsake you." Hebrews 13:5

11: A GREATER PLAN

They stood by his bedside and watched his body fade away. Just days before, he had been completely healthy with no symptoms whatsoever. But now, he would barely eat. The color in his face was slowly fading, and there was absolutely nothing that they could do to help him.

None of their usual home remedies would even touch his failing body. Despite their best efforts and relentless love, their brother was dying. And no one could help.

No one, that is – but Jesus.

They had sent for Him, but He had not yet come.

They knew that He could change things. He could heal him. He could save his life. They had been there when He had worked miracles like these for others.

They just needed Him, the Miracle-Maker to show up. To help. To heal. To come.

Jesus was actually a close friend of the family. They had spent many days traveling with Him, learning from His teachings, and serving others. They had shared meals together, laughing and talking about the things of hearts and lives and love. They deeply loved Him, and they knew that love was mutual. Which made it even more confusing as to why He had not yet arrived.

It just didn't make sense. He should have been here by now. Time was quickly running out. With every passing moment, Lazarus was becoming weaker. His every breath was strained.

She had lost count of how many times she had left his side to go to the door, to scan the long dusty road, silently praying that He would come soon.

Where could He possibly be?

What has happened that is taking so long?
What more could she possibly do?
Lord, please… don't take my brother.

They stood by his side, holding his hands in their own. With full hearts and saddened smiles, they told him how much that they loved him – how thankful they were that he was theirs.

They laughed as they shared childhood stories, reminiscing upon memories from long ago. Things that a few had forgotten – until this very moment.

With sorrow greater than they had ever known, they watched their treasured brother close his eyes and take his last breath, quietly slipping from this world to enter into another.

It had been four days since they had placed him in the tomb. None of this even seemed real, but as family and friends continued to come to express their sorrow and to pay last respects, they found it difficult to even pause and wonder how all of this came to be so quickly. He had not even been sick… and now, he was gone.

And to make matters worse… Jesus was still no where to be found. He loved Lazarus. They knew this. And He could have changed everything. But for some reason that they could not even begin to fathom, He had chosen to remain where He was. And to allow their beloved brother to die. Despite the fact that He had the power to prevent it all.

When Martha learned that Jesus was coming, she could not settle the rising entanglement of questions and emotions that seemed to consume her. Desperate for answers, to look Him, the Miracle-Maker directly in the eye and to ask Him why….. she ran out to meet him before he could even reach their home.

With anger laced in sorrow and tears of disappointment pouring, she looked at Him, her friend, their friend and asked the question that they had all wondered but could not ask – until now.

"Lord, if you had been here, my brother would not have died. But even now, I know that whatever you ask from God, God will give you." John 11:21-22

There. The words were spoken. What would He do with all of this grief? The One who could prevent it all, who could change it all now stood before her – after he was already four days deep in the tomb.

Though there was anger and questions and sorrow immeasurable, she could not reject the notion of knowing that somewhere deep within her soul – that this Miracle-Maker was still good. He was still trustworthy. He was still love.

Her questions did not negate His character.

Her emotions did not disqualify His loyalty.

Her lack of understanding did not remove His purpose.

He was still God in flesh – Emmanuel – God with us. Even though He chose to not come until now.

Precious one, His love for you, His goodness in heart, nature and motive is not contingent upon our belief in His goodness. He is good when we place our trust in Him. And He is still good when we choose to reject and deny Him. His Core, His Divine Spirit of love and grace and goodness cannot and will not be altered by our lack of belief.

Maybe you are one of the ones who has followed after Him your whole life. You fell in love with this Miracle-Man-God who fights demons and saves souls while eating goldfish crackers off a napkin and sipping red fruit punch while singing Jesus Loves Me with friends on a Sunday morning. Maybe you have grown up knowing His stories, memorizing His words of truth.

But now… forty years later… you find yourself sitting in ICU and watching your precious child battle for their very life. Maybe you have done everything you know to do to salvage the marriage, to win back his heart. But he longer wants you. The papers have already been drawn. Maybe you were the one who read all of the books, who attended classes and have done all that you can to wrestle your child away from danger and bring him back safely into your care. Regardless of your best efforts, he wants no part. So you find yourself calling the local prison to schedule visits behind a glass wall. Maybe you have served Him all of your life, and now you have been given a sentence - a death sentence by the test results in your hand. Two months ago you were deemed healthy – and now, your moments upon this earth are being numbered by the disease that has invaded your body and claimed your days.

Where is He in this?

Why hasn't He come?

If He has the power – the ability – the control to step in and intervene – to change worlds that we cannot even perceive, then where is this Jesus we sang to over kool aid and cheese crackers when we were five?

Where is He in the sorrow when it grieves us deeply to even breathe?

It is here that the Giver of Life, Miracle-Man-God gently whispers, "Precious one, I am here." "I will never leave you nor forsake you." Hebrews 13:5

Even and especially when we do not understand… He is here.

This Giver of Life and Lover of Souls is intensely woven into a world of glory that we simply cannot see. He has insight and vision and purpose – and it is all grounded and rooted on the premise and foundation of love.

He is working by a Master plan – a plan that we do not have access to. Because quite simply – He is God, and we are not. And while we prefer simple solutions, quick healing and painless answers, He is working towards a greater purpose – to bring empty hearts and wavering souls to come to know and trust Him.

The piece that Mary and Martha did not know is that it absolutely grieved His tender heart to stay where He was for those days. To not leave and be there. To not prevent this death. To not rescue these hearts of sorrow from unspeakable pain.

Yet, He knew that He was working for a greater purpose. It was part of the Master Plan. A plan that they could not see nor understand until a later time – when Glory would be revealed.

The heart of our Creator is never to drive us into pain and sorrow. Yet, He also knows that it is out of brokenness, unanswered questions and deep sorrow that His love is often revealed.

Because He is working towards an eternal purpose rather than a temporary one, He allows us to endure suffering so that our souls may be positioned towards the Giver of Grace and be made tender to receive His gift of relentless love and peace.

For it is in our brokenness, that His strength is made known. It is in our unanswered questions, fears and doubts that we come to truly know the comfort of His peace, the Giver of joy.

He is always working towards love - with the perfect plan in place. We simply must choose to trust Him. Like a five year old little one with our gold fish and red juice.

"I am the resurrection and the life. Whoever believes in me, though he die, yet shall he live, and everyone who lives and believes in me shall never die." John 11:26

12: YES, LORD…. I BELIEVE.

It grieved His heart to remain where He was at the time of Lazarus' greatest need. He knew that the entire family was anxiously awaiting for His arrival – to come and rescue them from their circumstances. But it wasn't time for Him to come. They wouldn't understand this, and He knew that. But He had to wait until the exact moment where the Glory, Goodness and Mercy of the Father could be truly seen.

He watched her as she came running out of the house to meet Him. Lazarus had already been in the tomb for four days – and this precious one was so distraught. She had so many questions. So many tears. If only she could see… that it grieved His heart too. If only she could see how much He loved Lazarus… how much He loved all of them.

He could attempt to explain His reasoning for staying so long – for not arriving until now – but sometimes, answers cannot be given for works on the other side of Heaven.

Though she was angry at this untimely death, He needed her to come to the place of trust, to the place of belief so that He could do His greatest works.

He had already told her that her brother would rise again. (John 11:23)

She thought that He was referring to the Resurrection of bodies that will happen on the Last Day. She truly did not know that He had a plan greater than what she could even comprehend. A plan to bring hope from the very ground.

Emmanuel, God-with-us smiled ever so gently at her. He absolutely loved this precious one! Even in her great sorrow, she still believed! He just needed her to see this great faith, this spiritual strength that lived within her soul. For even faith the size of a mustard seed can move mountains and transform lives.

Gently, He spoke these words, "I am the Resurrection and the Life. Whoever believes in Me, though he die, yet shall he live, and everyone who lives and believes in Me shall never die. Do you believe this?"

Do you believe this?

Do you believe Me?

These are the hard core questions of faith. When we are in a place where we can see no other way and hope seems to have completely locked us out... this is when Emmanuel, God-with-us meets us in our darkest hours and most turbulent days.

Do you believe this?

Do you trust Me?

And with every morsel of seed-faith that she could find tucked away behind anger, sorrow, and sheer exhaustion, she firmly spoke, "Yes, Lord, I believe that You are the Christ, the Son of God who is coming into this world." John 11:27

Yes, Lord.... I believe... even when I do not have all of the pieces. Even when I do not understand.

Yes, Lord... I believe... that You can bring hope and healing out of the ground.

Yes, Lord...I believe... that You are who you say you are. That you are loving and kind and good... that You have a redeeming plan.

Yes, Lord... I believe. I believe.

It is here where soul-fire lives. The power of faith – of believing without sight. This is where we must trust when we don't have clear answers, and we simply choose to rest in promises of our God. Completely blind.

It is here that He calls us to speak our belief, to proclaim our trust, to declare our faith. Because this is the prerequisite – the ground work of miracles – Heaven's fingerprints on earth. This is the conversation that we must have before anything else can be done. For faith is the fuel that activates God-movement. Without it, He cannot do the things of His heart.

With our every "Yes, Lord, I believe," we give Him permission to activate His supernatural Spirit, His undeniable power into the very broken places of our lives and to resurrect the hopes and dreams that we have laid to rest.

With our every "Yes, Lord, I believe," we give Him access to the most painful places in our lives – to the most damaged relationships and to the most severe wounds that have not yet healed.

With our every "Yes, Lord, I believe," we offer Him our ideas of how we think things should have happened or how He could have prevented it… and we release our accusations and judgments of Him for unyielding trust in His goodness and grace. Even and especially when we do not understand His ways.

With our every "Yes, Lord, I believe," we invite Him to come and create order out of chaos and beauty from all of the rubble left from our very broken lives.

Precious one, this Love-Giver, Life-Redeemer never… not once… looked at Mary and Martha and asked them not to grieve. He never reprimanded them for their questions or rebuked them for being disappointed. He did none of these things.

What He did do… was ask them to believe.

Even in the pain.

Even in the questions.

Even when they did not understand His plan or know why He had chosen to wait.

He asked them to believe.

And He is asking us to do the same. He is asking to trust Him when our world is caving in and we can no longer hold it together or even pretend that we are ok. He is asking for us to believe that He is the Great I Am, the Giver of all good things… and if He has waited (what you and I have deemed as too long) and He has allowed tragedy to occur and people to die or hearts to be crushed… even and especially here… He is asking for our hearts to still believe.

Beautiful one, there will be questions still unanswered on this side of eternity. There will be pain and tragedy, heartache and sorrow. There will be evil and blood shed and sickness and death. Yet, we have a Love Creator and a Life Giver who breathes His grace into sorrow and offers redemption into a world that is plagued by sin. And with our every "Yes, Lord, I believe..." He offers us a beautiful glimpse of His Master Plan, His glory unfolding, His sacred redemption gift...

"I have said these things to you, that in Me, you may have peace. In the world, you will have tribulation. But take heart; I have overcome the world." John 16:33

In our every "Yes, Lord... I believe," we are given the gift of peace. The promise of victory. The glimmer of hope.

In our every "Yes, Lord... I believe," we discover His heart in our sorrow, His presence in our pain, His comfort in our affliction and distress.

He is calling us into His Master Plan Design, creating beauty out of all of the brokenness... but it truly begins with us – our hearts – as we relinquish our desire to be god and humbly declare, "Yes, Lord... I believe."

"Daughter, your faith has made you well; go in peace, and be healed of your disease."

13: FAITH MADE WELL.

For twelve years, she had suffered with this. It was culprit of her isolation; every relationship she had previously enjoyed was now breached due to this condition. It was embarrassing. It was frustrating. It was disheartening to bare a disease that no one could seem to heal.

She had spent every dime that she owned on medical care, hoping for a resolution. Yet, every attempt was proven to be unsuccessful. The pouring of blood continued.

Never in her life had she been more desperate for help. Desperate for someone to come and make her well. To bring healing to her body and peace to her fragile soul.

Rumor had it that Jesus would be coming through her village. Somewhere deep within her core, she knew that this was an opportunity that she simply couldn't refuse or ignore. Others had been in His presence, and they had been healed.

She couldn't help but to question... if He could heal them, then why not her?

There were so many people surrounding Him in the dusty streets; she could barely even capture a glimpse of Him. There was simply no way possible that she would be able to reserve His attention.

But she knew that if she didn't act, there would be no hope. If she couldn't capture His Miraculous Hand, the bleeding would just continue. And every single day, she was getting worse.

With an act of desperation, she did the only thing that she knew to do... forcing herself into the crowd, she positioned herself just close enough where she would be able to reach out her hand

and grasp His garments. For she knew that if she could simply even touch His garments, that she would be made well. Mark 5:28

This Miracle-Man was now so close. With every bit of strength and focused determination that she could muster, she reached out to Him – and gently closed her eyes as His God-Gift-Grace poured from Him into her.

Immediately, she knew that it had truly worked; she had been healed! For her bleeding instantly ceased. There was a peace in her body and comfort in her soul that had not been present for years.

Perceiving the power that had left His body and poured into another, this Miracle-Man-God paused and turned to ask this massive crowd – Who was the one who reached out to Him in faith?

Called out for her act of desperation and faith intermingled into one, she approached Him in fear and trembling to share what she had done. The whole truth was now laid bare to see – this woman who was so desperate for relief.

And as she shared her heart, this Miracle-Man-God proclaimed, "Daughter, your faith has made you well; go in peace, and be healed of your disease."

So many of us are living in the cusp of desperation and faith all intermingled. With our every breath, we solemnly declare, "Yes, Lord… I believe." And still there are places in our lives that the bleeding – simply – will. Not. Stop. And we are desperate for answers. We are desperate for help.

For years, my son has battled mental illness. Wars within his heart and mind that lead to behaviors that make a mother's heart cringe and strangers fear.

We plead for his healing, deliverance of his mind.

Resources are poured out for testing, treatments, medications and counseling.

Yet, the bleeding continues. The mind-wars he continues to face. And it is here in this place, that too many of us stop believing. In the middle of the war zone, we simply lose hope.

Because what if He doesn't deliver to us in the same way that he delivered to her? What if we come in faith, expecting and believing for Him to answer our prayers in a specific way – to provide that healing, that deliverance, that miracle – but the answers that we receive are just not the answers that we want?

And so we question ourselves – wondering if our faith was too weak or was there some kind of wrong-doing (sin) in our lives that blocked our prayers from entering the throne of Heaven? We wage war within ourselves and begin to question the goodness of our God-Creator because He doesn't grant us the wishes of our hearts that we so desire.

Yet, what I am learning is this…. every single encounter with the Great I Am that is met with whole-hearted belief and trust in Him yields power in His touch. It just may look different than what we are expecting to receive.

In Isaiah 55:8-9, He firmly tells us, "For my thoughts are not your thoughts, neither are your ways my ways, declares the Lord. For as the heavens are higher than the earth, so are my ways higher than your ways and my thoughts than your thoughts."

For some, the bleeding may instantly be healed so that His glory can be seen and revealed – shared in ways that others come to know Him, the Soul-Redeemer.

Yet, for others, the story may look different. The bleeding may not immediately stop. The child who battles mental illness may endure this throughout his life. The circumstances that you cannot resolve may not be magically, miraculously erased in the way that we so desire. Yet, it doesn't mean that we are loved less or not as valuable as another. It simply means that He is working with the Master Plan – the One that we are not allowed to see. The one that we do not know. But it's written in the blood of the sacrifice from the Lamb; it's written with the ink of Love.

Even in the psychiatric hospital behind locked doors and confined rooms, the touch of Power is present. Even in the jail cell with prison mates and raw memories of wrongs committed – the touch of Power is present.

It was 4:00pm, and I was there to visit my son. He had just been committed (once again) to the psychiatric ward. But as I arrived to wait for my turn to be called back, the wailing screams began. Rage lashed out. The doors to the unit shook. Doctors were called. Back up was enlisted. Restraints were enforced and high dosage medications were administered. And I watched through tears and immense fear as the entire psychiatric ward of the hospital was closed off due to my son. My son. The one that I had birthed and loved. The one that I tried to safeguard from harm. The one that I could not protect against himself. Because of his erratic behavior and dangerous rage, no one was deemed safe. The doors were secured by men in uniforms, and all of the unit was locked down.

As the doors closed, I was left on the other side. With so many questions. Wondering how I could have possibly failed him to this extent. What did I do that was so wrong that it would end up like this? With a 10 year old boy shackled to a bed and strangers in uniforms with weapons on their hip, protecting the world from him.

And it was there – at this exact moment – in the deepest grief that I looked up and saw my baby brother walking in the door. Love coming to be present in the pain. Comfort coming to share the burden of grief.

The Grace-Giver's power released.

Precious one, He may not always remove the thing that causes us the most pain. He may not always heal that continuous bleeding that causes us shame. But what He does promise is that He will never leave us nor forsake us. He will meet us in that place. He will guide us, comfort us, encourage us, equip us, and restore us.

And He will use this story – this brokenness to truly make us well, to restore our souls, to make us whole. He will place people in our lives to share the burden and to carry us in prayer. He will use every piece of all the fragments of our lives – the things that we cannot understand – for the good.

We must simply declare, "Yes, Lord….. I believe" and move close enough to Him that we can reach out in the desperation and touch Him, knowing and believing that in His way, in His perfect plan, His power will be released.

"The man who had died came out, his hands and feet bound with linen strips, and his face wrapped with a cloth. Jesus said to them, "Unbind him and let him go." John 11:44

14: BRINGING THE DEAD BACK TO LIFE

After thirteen years of marriage, we had simply arrived at a dead end. Promises had been broken. Trust had been lost. So many broken pieces were scattered. Fragments of love, family, and once happiness had now come down to this….

Boxes packed in rooms.

The sorting of pictures and household things.

Questions from tearful, hurt children who understood none of these things.

Judgment from the outside world and family who disapproved.

Yet, in my heart, I knew that this was the very thing that I had to do. Despite what others may have believed or perceived, this was truly the very best thing that I could do for my own heart and for my precious children. To refuse to continue to wear the mask that everyone else wanted, but simply was not real.

Counseling had been attempted numerous times. Multiple meetings with spiritual leaders, counselors and friends – prayers over coffee, guidance sought at the crack of dawn. All of these things had been done. My urgent heart begged the Heart of Heaven to reveal the direction that I needed to proceed, and with every step I took, a door was opened. Things that I knew were true gifts – experiences that could only be truly delivered by the Grace Giver. And with every box I packed, the peace simply filled my heart.

Regardless of any outside opinion or unsolicited advice, deep within my heart, I knew and believed that the Grace-Giver was diligently working on my behalf, on my heart to bring the dead back to life.

It is when the stench of death is present – when the world that
we see and know has pronounced it all dead – and all that is left is
decaying dreams, mourning and sorrowful tears – this is the where
the Sustainer of Life and the Giver of Hope can be best seen.
Because up until this very moment, we thought that we could
somehow change things. We thought that we could alter the
direction of his someone else's decisions or counteract the hand of
Heaven. But here... where we are left with only our memories and
shattered dreams, we are forced to forfeit our wishes for His
dreams, our hopes for His heart.

There was absolutely no hope left when He walked into the
door of their home. Their precious beloved brother had already
been dead for days. For four days, he had already stayed in the
tomb.

Though they knew that He was the Christ, the Giver of Life...
nothing could help them understand or prepare for the miracle that
they so desperately wanted to receive.

She fell at His feet, bitter tears dripping upon His exposed,
sandy toes. With mourning pouring from her lips, she heard the
words of her heart at the exact moment that He also did... "Lord,
if you had been here, my brother would not have died."

The pain was simply unbearable. Though she loved Him, Jesus,
their beloved friend, she simply could not comprehend why He
would not have arrived sooner than this.

The grief in the room was stifling. And as He listened to her
heart-cries and heard the desperate sobs of the others mourning
this precious one, He found His own spirit grieving. Precious
Lazarus.

Asking where his friend had been placed, The Beloved Giver
of Life, Creator of Love began to weep tears of His own.

Precious one, please do not miss this. Please do not miss these
last words.

Asking where his friend had been placed, The Beloved Giver
of Life, Creator of Love began to weep tears of His own.

Precious one, He is present in the pain.

He is with you while the boxes are being packed or while you
watch your loved one choose to walk away.

He is with you while you are sitting beside a hospital bed, praying to the Heavens for a life to be spared.

He is with you at 2 am when you are waiting by the door, anxiously awaiting for your rebellious teenage daughter to walk in the door.

He is with you when the stench of hopelessness is all that you can smell and the tears will simply not stop pouring out – no matter how hard you try to hold them back.

He is present with you in all of this.

Every single bit of it. Emmanuel – God with us – is there in the midst.

And His love, passion, mission, and desire is the same purpose for you and for me as it was with Lazarus…. As He, the Miracle-God-Man calls the dead to rise!

Proclaiming the words of power with the authority from the Father and spoken through the Giver of Life, "Lazarus come out."

"Unbind him and let him go."

Beautiful girl, He is calling us out!

He is calling us out of our brokenness and into His wholeness.

He is calling us out of our chaos and into His peace.

He is calling us out of our anxiety and into His rest.

He is calling us out of our unanswered questions and into trusting Him!

He is calling us out of our present that we cannot change and into His beautiful, gracious, Master Plan!

He is calling us out of our shame and into His grace.

He is calling us out of our insecurity and loss of belonging and into knowing and believing that we are truly, genuinely His own!

He is calling us out of the accusing voices that we cannot seem to silence and the whispers of doubt that we cannot seem to bury… and He is calling us out of all of this – so that we may come to know ourselves. This woman of beauty that He has so delicately designed – before we ever even took our first breath. This woman of strength, grace, and joy. This woman who has been destined to change the world!

And as the strips of fear, insecurity, unworthiness, and shame are all stripped away, unbound from our hearts and lives…. We have the chance to meet her. The one that He watches from Heaven with joy in His heart and pride in His eyes... the one that He has been refining and restoring and healing – even when was completely unaware. The one that He delights over and rejoices in her heart! Let me introduce you to her..... this precious Daughter of Worth!

"But you are a chosen race, a royal priesthood, a holy nation, a people for his own possession that you may proclaim the excellencies of him who has called you out darkness into his marvelous light." 1 Peter 2:9

15: REDEEMED

I stood before the GLAM girls (the name that we have for Daughters of Worth mentorship group – which is an acronym for "Girls Living a Mission) and was completely covered in "My name is" labels. Each label shared a part of my story. A part of my history. A piece of my identity. Words that I had carried deep within my soul for as long as I could remember. The words that I had allowed for many years to claim my identity.

A mistake.
Product of an affair.
Unwanted.
Family secret.
Orphan.
Foster child.
Adopted.
Daughter.
Sister.
Niece.
Granddaughter.
Insecure.
Not pretty enough.
Not popular.
Deeply wounded.
Not smart enough.
Not athletic enough.
Not good enough.
Creative.

Writer.
Loves to give to others.
Scared.
Poor relationships.
Unwed mother.
Fear of failure.
Married at 20 years old.
No clue what I am doing.
Mom of 3.
Student (again).
Failed marriage.
Divorced.
Disappointed family and friends.
Single mom.
Barely enough to make ends meet.
No more masks.
No more days of pretending.
Still passionate to serve others.
Still. Just. Not. Enough.

These were the words that I had marked as mine. I proclaimed this as my story because it perfectly and simply defined the life that I had lived and known.

As I shared from my heart, these precious girls stared with eyes wide open and leaned forward, intent to hear the next piece that I would share. All of the preconceived notions that they had formed prior to this night about me and my life – was suddenly ripped to shreds. My life was absolutely nothing that they had once believed it was. You could see the look in their beautiful eyes.

With their devoted attention, I then shared with them – the words that I wish someone had spoken to me. At the age of 7. At the age of 12. At the age of 15. At the age of 19. At the age of 26. At the age of 30. At the age of 35.

Beautiful girl, your past does not define you.

Your worth is not based on your beauty, your intellect, your assets, or your life story. Your

Your limitations do not disqualify you for love, and your past mistakes do not reject you from the gift of grace.

Precious one, through the eyes of the Grace-Giver, the Love-Creator, the Life-Sustainer…. The only label that you have been given is this one:

Redeemed.

In Psalm 103:1-4, we are given these treasures of truth:

"Bless the Lord, o my soul, and all that is within me, bless his holy name! Bless the Lord, o my soul, and forget not all his benefits, who forgives all your iniquities, who heals all your diseases, who redeems your life from the pit, who crowns you with steadfast love and righteousness."

The Love-Creator does not exist to mock, shame, reject, and condemn. His entire premise is unconditional love and grace – to open the Door for those who are seeking eternal hope and to be rescued from the pit. Not only the pit of destruction – but the pit of our lives. The pit that we cannot change. The pit that we cannot remove. The pit that we cannot seem to crawl out of, despite our best efforts and continuous attempts.

Precious one, He is calling us out of the places that we have been. He is drawing us close to His heart where the echoes of the voices that we cannot silence begin to fade away as He invites us to come and sit quietly with Him. Here, in this place, we are reminded by His Divine Spirit that He alone is our Live Giver and Soul Redeemer. The changes that we desire, the life that we need to be mended and the relationships that need to be restored – these are the things that we simply do not have the power to transform on our own, through our efforts or persistent attempts. These are the things – the places of war within our souls – the pit that we fight against each and every day – these are the things that He is calling us to surrender. Bringing it all to His feet.

And as we are willing to allow Him to unbind us from all of the labels that we have been wearing, declaring and believing based on our past history or judgments from others or even judgments from ourselves, we begin to find freedom. We begin to breathe in peace.

One by one, the labels that we have been wearing quietly begin to disappear. Through His relentless mercy and gift of grace, we are no longer held captive by our past or mistakes.

We are given a new beginning.

A new day.

A new hope.

A new name.

A new life.... As the ashes begin to gather to form a new creation.

Something different...

Something unique...

Something that we have never experienced until now.

The place where the glimmer of light shines in our darkest wounds and the beginning of something beautiful and glorious begins to take root.

But it has taken until now – this very moment – for any of this to be revealed.

Because ashes cannot rise to beauty until we are willing and ready to surrender the loss, to trust in the Love-Giver and to rise up when called.

Ashes cannot rise to beauty until faith becomes more than words and we are willing to forfeit our carefully laid our plans for His Master Design.

Beautiful one, ashes cannot rise to beauty until we are willing to fall before His tender feet with hearts raw and vulnerable – authentically seeking Him.

Yet, at this very moment where we are ready and willing to place our hearts and lives into His Divine Hand,

It is here... in this very place... that He will call us out of the stench of the pit of our desperate lives... and begin to unbind us from our darkest wounds.

Labels begin to fall until the only thing left remaining is Him. The Miracle-Man-God in Flesh. Emmanuel. God with us.

His redeeming grace shining through all of the broken places of our lives where the glimmer and promise of hope shines so beautiful, so bright as this precious woman begins to rise with joy, confidence, and peace.

And it has nothing to do with her.

And it has everything to do with Him.

For she is just beginning to truly understand the beautiful, glorious, precious gift that He offers to her... her true identity as a Beloved Daughter of the King.

"Many Samaritans from that town believed in him because of the woman's testimony, "He told me all that I ever did." John 4:39

16: COME AND SEE

She had come thirsty.

With shame that haunted her, isolation that mocked her and questions about her life that she couldn't even begin to answer.

Yet, the day that she met Him, everything changed. The one who had the power and the authority to judge her heart, to judge her life, to cast her aside... did everything... but this.

The Love-Creator, Grace-Giver had waited for her to arrive. He had waited in the scorching heat for the exact moment that He knew that she needed to be redeemed.

While others shamed her, He embraced her.

While others isolated her, He invited her.

While others rejected her, He welcomed her.

And it was this... this authentic, ever-present Love that simply changed everything!

In the very moment that she realized who He truly was – the Messiah – Emmanuel – God with us, she knew that she could hide no longer. Others needed to know.

This story had to be shared – so that others could come to Him, the Eternal Well, the Living water of Life and find the gift that satisfies every longing thirst for completion, wholeness, and peace.

A woman who came thirsty for the water of the land leaves her empty jar at this very well – to go back into the very village that hours before, she had desperately tried to avoid. And all of this, to share these words.....

"Come and see."

Come and see...

Beautiful one, your story is a gift and it beckons to be told. Because the truth is… we are all broken. We are all raging against some battle, some war that attempts to rob us of our peace and to revoke our joy.

Yet, whatever place we are in – whatever that thing is that keeps you lying awake at night or holding your breath during the light of day, the Grace-Giver is waiting for us… just like He waited for her. The place where we are most thirsty. The place where we are most exhausted. The place where we are trying our best to escape the crowds and to isolate ourselves from the judgment of others. He is there. Waiting at the well.

As this precious one encountered the true Messiah and in Him found authentic love and genuine grace, the opinions of others immediately lost their value. Their judgments, criticisms, and shame were all pushed off the pedestal – so that she could welcome the sweet arms of Grace. For now that she had truly met the One who could wholeheartedly see into every corner of her life and chose to not condemn her – but rather to welcome her. To wait for her. To invite her. To encourage her. To love her – despite all of her flaws. This is the place that everything changed.

And this is the kind of love story that needs to be told.

This is the kind of love story that we have waited all of our lives to receive.

The one that we are so desperately wanted – treasured – cherished – that the Lover of our Souls would wait for us in our deepest need and to deliver us from the pit. Precious one, this is the Love that we have been holding our breath for and dreaming of since we were little girls. And it's not found in the arms of a Prince charming, but rather in the arms of the King. The Grace Giver. The Love Creator. The Great I Am.

And she discovered Him! Here at the well….

With a heart overflowing and peace consuming her every breath, she knew that she had to share this gift with others! And so, she ran back to the very place that she had once avoided… to speak of this Miracle-Man-God, this new Love found. To offer the invitation… This Man… He told me everything about my life… This One… could truly be the Christ!

Beautiful one, I don't want you to miss this! Please don't miss this!

The Creator of Love used the heart and life story of this thirsty woman to bring hearts to Emmanuel, the Soul-Redeemer. He used her. He used the woman who had been married 5 times and was now with another man. And they were not yet married. He used her. The woman who was shunned in the market place, who was gossiped about in the village. The woman who was the outcast. The woman who was rejected, mocked, and shamed.

This woman.

This woman is the one that He chose to wait for.

This woman is the one that He chose to reveal Himself to – so that she could truly see – how much she was loved.

And as her heart was healed, delivered from shame and regrets… as her soul was restored and her hope was renewed, she found herself passionately going back to share the gift of the Love Creator.

John 4:42 declares these powerful words:

"They said to the woman, "It is no longer because of what you have said that we believe, for we have heard for ourselves, and we know that this indeed the Savior of the world.""

Because this woman was willing to share her heart, her story, her encounter with the Messiah, lives were forever changed! Souls were redeemed.

Because she was willing to allow the joy and light of the new hope that she had discovered pour through her brokenness so that He could be seen, the people of the village came to know Him, their Creator and Savior!

Sweet girl, your story has tremendous power. And it needs to be told. For it is in our brokenness that His glimmer of hope is best seen. It is in our weakness that His strength is made known.

It is in our story that the world begins to see how the Love-Creator and the Grace-Giver takes the dusty ashes of our broken lives and breathes grace and life into it all – creating something new and absolutely beautiful that only He can do.

And as we begin to share the deep places of our hearts, our deepest wounds and His relentless love through it all… we too, will find that others will say... it is because of your story, that I came to the well. And it's no longer because of what you have said that I believe.... For He has made Himself known to me. Indeed, He is my Soul-Redeemer!

"Being confident of this, that He who began a good work in you will carry it to completion until the day of Jesus Christ." Philippians 1:6

17: REDEFINING NORMAL – ANOTHER PIECE HEALED

There are those people who enter your life – and once they do, you are simply changed. In ways that you cannot even explain. You just are. And for me, Rena Keith is certainly one of these people. Approximately 16 years ago, I had the privilege of meeting this phenomenal woman for the very first time. I will never forget hearing her heart spilled out in song, words, testimony, and tears from the stage.

A woman so beautiful.

So broken.

So powerful.

So strong.

So humble.

So empowering.

Throughout the years, this precious one has continued to inspire me in my own journey, as well as pour into the lives of countless others.

While writing this book, I knew that her story was one that needed to be shared... as this beautiful one lives out her faith in the Love-Creator daily through her own redemption story of shattered dreams rising to hope and beauty.

When she opened her eyes on the morning of May 7, 2004, her entire world had changed. A life of traveling, singing, and ministry with her two best friends was suddenly revoked as the startling reality of a true nightmare became her life... a nightmare that she has never been able to awaken from.

The bond that Rena' and Carla shared was formed by the absolute heartstrings of the Love-Creator. From high school to college days, they were simply inseparable.

Secrets had been whispered and stored, memories tucked away, jokes remembered, hopes and dreams treasured. In a place where best friends can truly become soul mates – this is the place that Rena' and Carla shared.

I giggled as she shared that even after they were each married, they would still call the other to simply say good night.

For those of us who have ever dreamed of having a sister of heart, this friendship is indeed what they were blessed enough to find in this life!

Yet, every dream that had been built, every hope that had been stored was suddenly ripped apart at the seams as a car accident redirected the entire course of their lives.

It was a back, windy country road in North Carolina and signs that were not well displayed to warn drivers. In a matter of moments that seemed like eternity, the car became under the control of a pile of sand that was blocking the road way.

Piercing screams were yelled as their fragile bodies were tossed, crushed, and chopped away by the harsh force of metal against bones. Asphalt against flesh.

Ribs were broken. Lungs were punctured. Blood poured out. Bodies were misconfigured. In a matter of moments – everything had completely changed. The lives that they had previously known were forever dismantled. Ashes of once-held-tight-dreams were all that remained.

The sound of sirens filled the quiet country road as emergency personnel arrived to the scene and air flights were scheduled to Duke University Hospital. Family members were urgently called in – with no real promise to hang onto.

"Rena is in critical condition," they whispered. "You will just have to wait."

Tears were loudly wept in the waiting room and urgent prayers filled the Heavens by family and friends and the community whom she loved, and whom loved her.

Prayers that begged the Giver of Grace and the Creator of Life to please save her. Please spare her life. Their beautiful, precious baby girl.

Significant damage had been executed on her left leg. With every flip of the car, her precious leg had been caught outside of the door – cutting and chopping away her muscles and bones.

The immediate prognosis delivered was to begin reconstructive procedures to her face – and they also suggested for the family to approve the amputation of her left leg.

Yet, Rena's daddy, a pastor with Pentecostal fire and faith that cannot be quenched refused for his baby girl's leg to be removed.

Surgeon upon surgeon left his presence, all with the same recommendation. And with love in his heart and fierce daddy strength, he kindly sent them all away. They were down to the last one – the fifth one, to be exact. He was firmly instructed that whatever this one said... they would have to comply. Too much was at stake.

The fifth one proclaimed that he too, felt it was best to amputate. However, if they chose to resist... he was confident that he could indeed, save her leg. He just couldn't promise what the outcome would be. He was not able to declare that this leg would ever be functional for her to walk again.

A man of deep conviction and filled with the daddy protection somberly declared, "Thank you, Doctor. Thank you! You do your part. God will do His."

In a matter of hours, a life that had once been filled with vibrant plans, beautiful dreams, and a friendship that others could only long for was left in a heap of ashes – directly beside the road's pile of unwarned sand.

As Carla left this world to enter another – the place of Eternal love, hope, and grace – Rena' was waking up to a cold hospital room. With pain in her body. With questions that she could not answer. Without her best friend.

Only pain, tears, sorrow, grief, remorse, guilt were the ones to meet her here. Or at least that is what she felt.

Yet, the Creator of Love and the Giver of Grace was already there. Protecting her. Loving her. Guiding her. Directing her. Even when she had no idea that He was even there.

In 2 Corinthians, chapter 12, Paul shares how he has this thorn in his side – this thing that constantly torments him. Continuously, he asked for the Soul-Redeemer to remove this thorn. Yet, for reasons that we do not know, the request was simply not granted.

However, Paul is not left without any answer. He is given these words by the Life-Creator, the Lover of our Souls:

"My grace is sufficient for you for my power is made perfect in weakness."

Precious one, do not miss these words!

My grace is sufficient for you.

My grace is sufficient for you.

When our dreams are turned into ash and our plans have vanished in hours… when our soul mate has stopped breathing and our bodies are crushed…. His grace is sufficient. His grace is sufficient.

Because His Magnificent Designer Plan does not always appear in the way that we desire or expect, it is so simple for us to conclude that He has neglected His promises.

Yet, as He pursues His eternal Designer-Plan, we begin to capture a glimpse of hope rising, new dreams being created and beauty from ashes being born.

There isn't a day that passes that Rena' does not long for her beloved friend or reflect on the joy-filled moments that was once the life that she knew and adored.

Yet, as the Creator of Life and the Giver of Grace slowly began to heal and restore her soul, she has learned that even in our deepest tragedies and most painful wounds – the Lover of our Souls is still good.

In the place of extreme brokenness, He is using her story to bring hope and healing in a way that is completely new. And as she shares her story, another wound begins to heal.

In her blog, "Redefining Normal," Rena shares these words:

I have been in awe so much the past few months. For thirteen years, I have only been able to see me as broken. I have stood in the middle of my fragmented life. I have looked down and seen the pieces laying around me. I picked up the pieces I could and tried to piece as much of me back together as I could. Or so I thought, that was all that was happening.

But sitting at a stop sign at the end of my neighborhood on a Tuesday morning in July, my spirit heard, "Rena', I have healed another piece of you." I didn't even realize it was happening, but I could see it. I could feel it. I still had a purpose greater than myself.

I have a testimony to tell. I know what it is like to long for what use to be, wishing things could be normal again. I know what it is like to try and recreate your own normal. And now, He has brought me to a place where I can truly say, I'm ready to see how He defines my life."

Beloved one, the same Giver of Grace who has given Rena' the ability to walk and the strength to serve children as a school counselor and the inspiration to share her story through her blog and speaking engagements is the same One who has the power and ability to rewrite your story!

In the place where all we can see is what was – what has been – what we wanted to be – the Designer of Hearts and the Creator of future whispers into our souls…

My grace is sufficient for you.

There is a plan, and it is beautiful.

I can and will use you in your weakness and in your pain.

You simply must trust Me.

Rely upon Me and allow me to direct your steps.

I will lead you to place of abundant joy and peace that exceeds your understanding.

Trust in Me…

And I will restore the years that you thought were lost

And the dreams that you once held so dear.

I will do a new thing in you – if you simply allow Me to do so.

And it will be beautiful and glorious…

As the ashes of your life fade away and beauty rises like the sun.

Beloved one, you will have a new song in your heart and a story that beckons to be told.

For this is the work that I desire to do in you.

To heal - yet another – piece of your soul.

The Spirit of the sovereign Lord is on me, because the Lord has anointed me to proclaim good news to the poor.

He has sent me to bind up the broken hearted, to proclaim freedom for the captives and release from darkness for the prisoners, to proclaim the year of Lord's favor and the day of vengeance of our God, and to comfort all who mourn,

And provide for those who grieve in Zion – to bestow on them

A crown of beauty instead of ashes,

The oil of joy instead of mourning, and a garment of praise instead of a spirit of despair.

They will be called oaks of righteousness, a planting of the Lord for the display of his splendor.

Isaiah 61:1

"Now to Him who is able to do far more abundantly than all that we ask or think, according to the power at work within us" Ephesians 3:20

18: FROM ASHES TO BEAUTY RISING

I remember the exact moment that I began praying this specific prayer.

The boys were so little, and I quickly learned that one of the few I places I could find refuge as a stay at home mom was in the bathroom.

It was often soaking in a hot, bubble bath that I would find a few moments of quiet and my heart would be able to be still long enough to hear the whisper of the Heavens.

On this particular day, everything in my entire life seemed to be caving in, and the only thing that I could do was sink deeper into the hot, soapy bubbles and give the tears permission to fall.

There were so many battles that I could no longer fight. There were so many questions that I simply could not answer. It was as if everything that I had known was absolutely falling apart – and there was nothing that I could do to stop the destruction.

And as I reached the place where there were simply no more words left to pray… these were the heart cries that I heard my soul whisper next…

"Lord, please just let my life count. Let it count for more than just my family – for more than my home. Let it count for more than my community. Let it count for the nations… for the kingdom. Please, just let my life somehow matter. Please, just let my life count."

And for the past fifteen years, this has been my heart cry, my soul whisper to the Heavens… that my life would count. It is only because of His great mercy and relentless love that He has chosen to answer – to allow there to be some kind of beauty rising from all of the dusty ashes – from all of the broken pieces in my life.

Precious one, regardless of the place that you are in at this exact moment, I want to encourage you that He is creating something glorious and absolutely beautiful out of all of the mess – and it will absolutely exceed anything and everything that you could even begin to possibly imagine!

In 2015, there was a vision – a passion – a mission that the Grace-Giver and Dream-Creator placed in my heart. I had been working with girls of all ages for approximately 15 years and could tell you story upon story of their hearts, their battles, their struggles, their wars. Depression. Attempted suicides. Homelessness. Poverty. Girls who had been raped. Pregnancy. Abortions. Cutting. Self-mutilation. Girls who hated themselves. Girls who had been sold to pay their mother's rent. Story upon story. Life upon life. Heart upon heart. And it wasn't just one community, one city, one county, or one school. There were so many girls who simply did not know what they were even worth.

In the midst of my own family wars and battles for my own peace, the Love-Creator placed in my heart a vision that I simply could not resist. A vision to create a unique mentorship program for the girls of our communities – providing her with a safe haven of support – while, we – her strong tribe of women surrounded her with love to empower her life!

I did not have all of the answers. There was no funding set aside for this sort of endeavor, and to be completely honest… I had no idea where or how to even begin. But what I do know is that when the Love-Creator and Grace- Giver places a dream in your heart and a vision in your life, it is for His purpose and it is to transform lives! If it is truly of Him, it is something that you will not be able to let go.

Through the support of family and friends, Daughters of Worth was incorporated as a non-profit organization! It was nothing but incredible to watch this vision begin to take root and for this organization to begin serving the girls of Pitt County!

Yet, as my life began to unravel with desperate children in need of medical attention, psychiatric assistance and run-ins with the law, I could not understand why I was the one with this vision for Daughters of Worth. How was I supposed to help these precious girls when I was incapable of handling my own children? How could I possibly pour into them when my own flesh and blood needed things that I could not even begin to offer?

And as I questioned the Maker of the Universe, the Love-Creator to explain all of this…. Wondering if I should just simply walk away from it all… with tears flooding and my heart crushed in desperation, I whispered my life prayer just once more… "Just please, Lord, make my life count."

Silence.

This.

This was the moment for me.

If there was ever a moment in my life that I have been absolutely certain of the voice of my God and the calling upon my life – this was it.

These were the words that I received:

Do you not see? Do you not hear? Do you not understand what I have done?

For fifteen years, you have prayed daily – sometimes continuously for your life to count. For your breath to matter. Do you not realize that Daughters of Worth is an answer to that prayer?

You are not allowed to quit. You are not allowed to give up.

I am using your brokenness to pour hope into these girls.

To walk away from Daughters of Worth is to rebuke the very thing that I have created you for and to rebuke the answer of your very own prayer.

I will never forget that moment.

Sitting silently in my car.

So humbled – so quiet – so shamed.

Never before had I realized that He was using all of the shattered pieces, broken promises and chaos of my life to lead me to the dreams and prayers of my heart.

While one son sat behind a prison cell with orange clothing on his back, another son sat in a psychiatric ward with a raging mind that I could not heal... and here... in this place of grief, tragic pain and loss, the Giver of Grace met me here. At my well.

Beautiful girl, if you are waiting for your family issues to be resolved before you step into the calling of your life... you may never take the first step.

If you are waiting for your heart to be healed, for your finances to be stable, for your life to settle down, more than likely, you will always be waiting.

There is never the perfect time or perfect way to step into the thing that He has called you to do. But your story is one of power – one that needs to be told.

His willingness to take our fragile, broken pieces and mold them into beauty and grace has nothing to do with our circumstances, but rather the willingness of our hearts.

He is willing, waiting, and ready for us to come and meet Him here. At the place where are souls are so thirsty for Living Water – for our parched hearts to be made well.

And there is this dream that He has created, designed for you and for your life! We simply must be willing to relinquish our pride, to surrender our shame and to grant Him access to our deepest wounds.

It is only here – in this place of trust-surrender – where we come to truly know the Grace Giver. And as we give Him every piece of broken promises and failed dreams, He will reveal the Masterpiece that He has long designed....

The place where ashes fade ...

And beauty will rise.

And the glimmer of His hope and glory can be seen

As we, beloved ones, choose to whisper once more...

"Yes, Lord.... I believe."

This is the place where you are invited to cuddle up with your warm, cozy blanket and hot cup of coffee and meet the Giver of Grace, the Lover of your Soul, and drink from the Living Water.

He is waiting for you by The Well.
Now begins your journey
To exchange your perception for His reality,
Your wishes for His dreams,
Your brokenness for His wholeness,
Your weakness for His strength,
Your ashes for His beauty.

Welcome, Beautiful Girl.
You are So Loved Here!
Welcome to The Well.

COME TO THE WELL

CHAPTER 1

With my every breath, I fully believe that there are hundreds of thousands of women who are just like me. They have been chained to the voice and lies of the enemy, locked in a mental and emotional prison. They are continuing to partake of the toxin directly from the hand of the enemy. And all because we have believed the lie.

What lie(s) have you believed, and how has it impacted your life?

So many women have tucked these beliefs into their soul that they are not loved, wanted, good enough, smart or enough or pretty enough. Just not enough. No matter how desperately hard they try. Have you ever fallen into this place? If so, how it affected your relationships, your confidence, your joy, your life overall?

Read Psalm 139. What part of this passage speaks to your heart? What are the truths that you need to be reminded of from the Grace-Giver?

In what ways do you believe that your life will change as you stop listening to the lies of the enemy and start receiving and believing the Truth of the Creator of Life?

COME TO THE WELL

CHAPTER 2

Psalm 139 proclaims, "Your eyes saw my unformed substance; in your book were written, every one of them, the days that were for me, when as yet there were none of them."

How does this truth impacts our hearts and lives?

Regardless of the fact that my blood line felt that they had to protect the name and ministry by keeping me a secret and placing me for adoption, my frame was truly Never hidden! His eyes saw me and knew me. He was devising a Master plan that would involve many more people, and this was all a part of His plan to fulfill His mission for the calling and purpose that He had poured into me. Even before the creation of the world!

Many of us have beginnings or story lines that cause deep pain. Yet, there is a hope when we know that in Him, we are never a mistake! In what ways (that you can see) has He orchestrated your family or story line to bring you to this place in life – to be used for His purpose?

We simply must allow His love to come and heal our deepest wounds and to silence the voice of the enemy through the power and authority of His truth.

What are the wounds that you need healed? What is the voice of the enemy that needs to be silenced through the Truth-Tellers?

COME TO THE WELL

CHAPTER 3

In the gut-wrenching crisis of failed dreams, robbed hopes, unplanned events, family secrets, shameful mistakes and detoured lives, it's incredibly easy for us to come to the conclusion that we must have really screwed up something significant to now be here – in this place.

Have you found yourself in this pit of shame? Believing that your past mistakes are the reasons why you are now in this place of desperation?

When we fail to realize that we have been created, stitched together with Love, it is nearly impossible to encourage others in the journey. If we are silently questioning His motives for our own lives, we are certainly going to struggle attempting to declare His goodness for others.

In what ways do you question your beginning – your life story? What are the silent places that you truly wonder about His motives for you and your life?

Read Jeremiah 29:11-13.

What truths of your Grace-Giver do you find in these passages?

What does this speak to our hearts of His plans, motives, and character?

COME TO THE WELL

CHAPTER 4

Too many times, we blame and accuse the Love-Giver, the Creator of our souls for our personal tragedies. We hold Him responsible for our unhappiness – for our failed plans and shattered dreams. Somewhere in the quiet place of our soul, we have attributed the Giver of Life with the character of the Taker of lives (the enemy.) Somewhere in the place of chaos and grief, we forget that God is actually good. And that He genuinely, authentically loves us – even and especially in the beautiful, broken places of our lives.

In what ways have you discovered that you are holding the Love-Giver for workers of the taker?

In His hands, we are safe and protected! We must choose to trust Him – even as we are surrounded by fragments of our lives, pieces that we have no clue what to do with or what they even are. All He wants is our hearts and our trust. And He will do the rest. We simply must invite Him to do so.

Romans 10:9-10 proclaims, "If you confess with your mouth that Jesus is Lord and believe in your heart that God raised Him from the dead, you will be saved. For with the heart one believes and is justified and with the mouth one confesses and is saved."

The Giver of Life and Love is not seeking people who are religious slaves. He wants our hearts. Relationship. Fellowship. For us to love Him and to love others. And as we learn that we can trust Him with our wounded hearts, we will position ourselves to be healed – to be restored.

COME TO THE WELL

CHAPTER 5

When was the last time that you experienced being in the "waiting room" of life?

Why do you think in places of suffering and grief that we suddenly find ourselves questioning the Love and Grace of our God?

Yet, as we attempt to rush the Creator of Life and Love or to move ahead of Him out of spite, we risk people getting hurt. We risk opportunities being missed. We risk the beautiful and profound moments that are birthed out of the mundane. The moments that we discount as inconsequential are many times the very moments where the weeds are being cut down to reveal the path in the wilderness. And if we rush by too quickly or run ahead of Him before the path has been cleared, we are at risk for missing the beauty that He is so graciously designing out of the broken. The masterpiece made from the remnants of tragedy.

Have you ever attempted to rush ahead of God to accomplish your plan or goal? What was the outcome?

Read Deuteronomy 8:11-6. Reflect on significant times that the Lord provided for you in a time of great need or fulfilled a promise to you. How does this remembrance impact our trust in Him?

In what ways have you experienced the difference between a life-giving relationship with the Giver of Grace rather than the soul-sucking, rule-following, not-enoughness that religion generates.

DRINK FROM THE WELL

CHAPTER 6

Read Isaiah 55:8-9.

As you read this passage, what are the places in your life that you simply need to trust the Creator of Love?

It is often easy for us to become "stuck" in a place of sorrow when we are consumed by our life's circumstances. In what ways have you experienced being stuck or consumed in brokenness?

Galations 5:1 proclaims, "For freedom Christ has set us free; stand firm therefore, and do not submit again to a yoke of slavery."

As you begin to drink from the well of freedom and restoration, the shackles of shame begin to fall away. What are the places in your heart that you need to be set free from?

DRINK FROM THE WELL

CHAPTER 7

When we place our identity in anything other than the Giver of Life and Creator of Love, we position ourselves for disappointed anxiety and fear. How does your view of yourself change as you acknowledge that your worth is defined by the Grace-Giver rather than all of the other things of your life?

Reflect on Philippians 4:8. How does this list compare to your actual thoughts? Why do you think that this was included in scripture? What value does it actually hold in your own life?

What are the voices of shame that you need to silence? What are the words of inadequacy and unworthiness that you need to bury indefinitely?

Refer to the Grace-Giver and the Love-Creator well of Living Water to find the scriptures that your heart is thirsty for – write them here.

DRINK FROM THE WELL

CHAPTER 8

Beloved one, so many times, we have this false notion that we cannot come and be with Jesus until we have all of our lives in order and all of the broken pieces are out of sight.
In what ways are you waiting for specific pieces of your life to be fixed before you come to the Well?

The Grace-Giver did not exclude the woman at the well because of her poor choices, current situation or circumstances. What ways do we fear that we will be disqualified or cast aside from the Creator of Love because of our brokenness?

The beauty of brokenness is the power that rests in its limitations, weaknesses and vulnerability. For when we are weak, He is strong. When we are at the end of ourselves and cannot find a way to calm the storm, we are in the perfect position for the Grace-Giver to do His best work!

How are you thirsty for His healing, for His restoration, for His power to redeem the broken places of you.

DRINKING FROM THE WELL

CHAPTER 9

Read and reflect on 1 Corinthians chapter 13.

This is the true definition of love given to us by the One whom created love. What are the truths of this passage that resonate in your heart? How does our culture's definition of love differ from this passage?

"Healing can only be given for those who truly desire to be made well. And beauty can only arise from ashes that are willingly released."

Are you at the place where you truly desire to be made well?

Are you at the place where you are willing to release the brokenness – the ashes to the Hands of the Redeemer so He can re-create your ashes into something beautiful?

If so, share your heart here…

TASTING THE LIVING WATER

CHAPTER 10

As we truly encounter the Love-Creator, the Grace-Giver, the Soul-Redeemer, how does He differ than the God of religion and laws that we are often taught?

What freedom of heart and hope of our soul is experienced when we truly meet Him – the One who desires to redeem, not condemn. The One who sacrificed everything – Himself included – to offer the opportunity for this gift of grace, eternal life?

In what ways do you identify with the woman who has been exposed in sin or the religious ones who are holding stones, waiting for the moment to spill her blood?

In what ways do we attempt to shame, mock, ridicule and murder the hearts of the exposed today?

TASTING THE LIVING WATER

CHAPTER 11

And to make matters worse... Jesus was still nowhere to be found. He loved Lazarus. They knew this. And He could have changed everything. But for some reason that they could not even begin to fathom, He had chosen to remain where He was. And to allow their beloved brother to die. Despite the fact that He had the power to prevent it all.

Have you experienced this place? Desperately needing Jesus to resolve a situation or restore relationships – and it feels as if He were no where to be found? If so, share your experience.

Read John 11:21-22.

In this passage, we hear the desperate plea, the confused tone of a woman who is grief-stricken. Yet, at the end of this passage she states, "But even now, I know that whatever you ask from God, God will give you."

How is she declaring faith in the Giver of Life through this statement?

What "But even now" statements do we need to proclaim to Him in our own lives?

Her questions did not negate His character. Her emotions do not disqualify His loyalty. Her lack of understanding did not remove His purpose. He was still God in Flesh – Emmanuel – God with us. Even though He chose to not come until now.

In what ways do you need to rest in His goodness rather than be tangled up in your own perspective? In what ways do you need to trust in Him – Emmanuel – God with us – for the places that you simply cannot understand?

Because He is working towards an eternal purpose rather than a temporary one, He allows us to endure suffering so that our souls may be positioned towards the Giver of Grace and be made tender to receive His gift of relentless love and peace.

How does our view change when we truly begin to believe that He is a good God, working things out through love – in accordance with the Master Plan of an eternal purpose?

TASTING THE LIVING WATER

CHAPTER 12

"Yes, Lord, I believe that You are the Christ, the Son of God, who is coming into this world." John 11:27

There is power that happens when we are willing to relinquish our questions for His plan… when we choose to simply believe and trust in spite of all the emotion, tears, and confusion. This where His love is most vividly seen.

This is your space. Your journal. You are here at the well

What are the "Yes, Lord, I believe" statements that you need to share with the Lover of Your Soul?

Gratitude Journal.

We may not understand any of what He is doing in our lives… but through our, "Yes, Lord, I believe," we can know that He is working towards the beautiful plan of His design, bringing ashes into beauty.

Spend time in this space today thanking Him for the work that He is already doing – that you are totally unaware of – and the work that He will do to fulfill His plan of Love.

TASTING THE LIVING WATER

CHAPTER 13

So many of us are living in the cusp of desperation and faith all intermingled. With our every breath, we solemnly declare, "Yes, Lord... I believe." And there are still places in our lives that the bleeding – simply – will. Not. Stop. And we are desperate for answers. We are desperate for help.

Are there places in your life that are bleeding profusely and you simply don't know how to make it stop? If so, share your experience.

Have you ever found yourself in the place of wondering if your faith was too weak, if there was sin blocking your healing or if you simply were not capturing His attention? If so, how does this impact your relationship and trust in the Giver of Life?

Read Hebrews 13:5.

How does the Promise of His Presence impact our trust in Him? In what ways does it bring peace into the chaos and light into the darkness – to simply know that He is present – that he is here – that He is working – even when we cannot recognize it on our own?

TASTING THE LIVING WATER

CHAPTER 14

It is when the stench of death is present – when the world that we see and know has pronounced it all dead - and all that is left is decaying dreams, mourning and sorrowful tears – this is where the Sustainer of Life and the Giver of Hope can be best seen, Because up until this very moment, we thought that we could somehow change things. We thought that we could alter the direction of someone else's decisions or counteract the hand of Heaven. But here…. Where we are left with only our memories and shattered dreams, we are forced to forfeit our wishes for His dreams, our hopes for His heart.

In what ways have you personally experienced this?

Just as Jesus, God-with-us wept tears for Lazarus – moved to sorrow at this temporary loss… He also shares in our pain. He is also present in our pain. In what ways have you experienced His presence in the most sorrow-filled moments in your life?

Beautiful girl, in the same way He called Lazarus – a decaying man – out of the tomb, He is calling us out of our decaying lives.

In what ways is He calling you out of brokenness and into healing – out of shame and into freedom? Share your heart.

BROKEN AND BEAUTIFUL

TASTING THE LIVING WATER

CHAPTER 15

What are the words that you have used to identify your heart – your story – yourself throughout the years?

How do these words differ than the ones the Grace-Giver offers to us?

Ashes cannot rise to beauty until we are willing and ready to surrender the loss, to trust in the Love-Giver and to rise up when called. Ashes cannot rise to beauty until faith becomes more than words and we are willing to forfeit our carefully laid out plans for His Master Design. Beautiful one, ashes cannot rise to beauty until we are willing to fall before His tender feet with hearts raw and vulnerable – authentically seeking Him.

What labels, beliefs, fears and emotions do you need to surrender or forfeit so that you can rise to beauty that He has called forth?
Are you willing and ready to let these things go?

What does it mean to you to know that you are truly a beloved daughter of the King and the only label that you need to own and proclaim is the one, "Redeemed?

INVITATION TO THE WELL

CHAPTER 16

A woman who came thirsty for the water of the land leaves her empty jar at this very well – to go back into the very village that hours before, she had desperately tried to avoid. And all of this, to share these words… come and see. Come and see.

Who was the person who introduced you to the Creator of Love and to the Giver of Grace?

How has your life been changed by meeting Him?

In what ways do you believe that your grace story beckons to be told? How can your brokenness – your experiences – your redemption story help others discover hope?

Sweet girl, your story has tremendous power. And it needs to be told. For it is in our brokenness that His glimmer of hope is best seen. It is in our weakness that His strength is made known. It is in our story that the world begins to see how the Love-Creator and the Grace-Giver takes the dusty ashes of our broken lives and breathes grace and life into it all – creating something new and absolutely beautiful the way that only He can do.

What is your story? How is He breathing the breath of life into your broken places? If you aren't quite sure what your story is yet, ask the Soul Redeemer to show you how He wants to use you – to use your story. Ask Him for guidance, for words, for opportunities.

INVITATION TO THE WELL

CHAPTER 17

"Being confident of this, that He who began a good work in you will carry it to completion until the day of Christ Jesus." Philippians 1:6

What does this passage-truth mean to you?
How does it impact how we view our daily lives and the broken places that are in need of healing-redemption?

Yet, as the Creator of Life and the Giver of Grace slowly began to heal and restore her soul, she has learned that even in our deepest tragedies and most painful wounds – the Lover of our Souls is still good.

In what ways can you declare His goodness in the midst of brokenness?

How does He use our stories of devastation and loss to bring hope and healing to others?

In what ways does it benefit others – as well as ourselves – to be willing to be transparent, authentic and willing to share the Grace stories of our broken and redeemed lives?

Invitation to the Well

Precious one, spend time today reflecting on this beautiful
passage – the call upon our lives to bring others to the well.
Color, draw, doodle, or simply pray. You choose how you
interact with these gift words from our Grace Giver and Soul
Redeemer.

"The Spirit of the Sovereign Lord is on me,
because the Lord has anointed me
to proclaim good news to the poor.
He has sent me to bind up the brokenhearted,
to proclaim freedom for the captives
    and release from darkness for the prisoners,
to proclaim the year of Lord's favor
    and the day of vengeance of our God,
to comfort all who mourn,
    and provide for those who grieve in Zion –
to bestow on them a crown of beauty
    instead of ashes,
the oil of joy
    instead of mourning,
and a garment of praise
    instead of a spirit of despair.
They will be called oaks of righteousness,
    a planting of the Lord
for the display of His splendor."
- Isaiah 61:1-3

HEALED FROM THE LIVING WATER OF THE WELL

CHAPTER 18

Precious one, regardless of the place that you are at in this exact moment, I want to encourage you that He is creating something glorious and absolutely beautiful out of all of the mess – and it will absolutely exceed anything and everything that you could even begin to possibly imagine!

Beloved, read Ephesians 3:20-21.

What is the promise and hope that you find in this passage?

Beautiful girl, if you are waiting for your family issues to be resolved before you step into the calling of your life – you may never take the first step.

If you are waiting for your heart to be healed, for your finances to be stable, for your life to settle down, more than likely, you will always be waiting.

There is never the perfect time or perfect way to step into the thing that He has called you to do. But your story is one of power – one that needs to be told.

In what ways have you been waiting for the "right time" to live out the dreams of your heart?

What are you learning about the place of your redemption story and its power of being told?

What is the "Yes, Lord…. I believe" that is necessary in your life for ashes to rise to beauty? For your life to be restored through the Love-Creator and the Grace-Giver?

97850645R00078

Made in the USA
Columbia, SC
18 June 2018